THE GREAT AMERICAN DRUMS

★ ★ ★ And The Companies That Made Them, 1920-1969

By Harry Cangany

Edited by Rick Van Horn

Design and layout
Scott G. Bienstock

Cover photo: 1938 Slingerland *Radio King* snare drum
Photo from the author's collection

Published By:
Modern Drummer Publications, Inc.
12 Old Bridge Road
Cedar Grove, New Jersey 07009 U.S.A.

★ ★ ★ ★ ★ ★ ★ ★

Acknowledgements

Dedicated To My Drum Heroes And Helpers

To Bill Ludwig, Jr.: My friend who let me into his world and made me a teenager again.

To Ben Strauss: The gentleman from Ohio who pushed Rogers into my life.

To Ringo Starr: Who got me ready to learn.

To Erwin Mueller: Who got me to learn.

To the late Ray Poland: For forty years of service to Leedy and a great service to me.

To the late Del Rowlinson: My parents' neighbor who first told me about Leedy drums.

To John Aldridge, Ned Ingberman, Jonas Aronson, Rob Cook, and Richard King: Who started me on the "Road to Collection."

To Ron Spagnardi and Rick Van Horn: Who helped turn this book from a dream into a reality.

…And to the hundreds of friends and acquaintances who have come into my life and enriched it by becoming a "Drum Friend."

Contents

Foreword

I'll never forget February 9, 1964. Along with millions of other teenagers and their curious parents, I watched the Ed Sullivan Show and saw the Beatles. About one second into their performance, I sat mesmerized by the experience. At the age of fourteen, I knew about Gene Krupa and Buddy Rich and remembered seeing them on television. But Ringo Starr called out to me through those invisible airwaves to pick up some sticks. Over the next three months, my mother took notice of my pleading and the promise to practice, practice, practice, and arranged a meeting with Erwin Mueller, the principal percussionist with the Indianapolis Symphony. He was a fine teacher and a superbly talented man, and I was a bit of a rebel, but he worked around that and for four years gave me warm instruction on man's oldest instrument.

Back in the '60s, most young drummers in my area fell into one of two armed camps. You were either a "Slingerland man" or a "Ludwig man." (I don't remember seeing any females playing drums at that time, so the term "man" could be used!) No self-respecting Ludwig man would be caught dead playing anything made by Slingerland, and vice versa. Sure, there were people playing on Camco, Gretsch, and Rogers, but they didn't count in the "drum war."

During a lesson with Erwin Mueller in 1964 I was told it was time to order my set. Out came the latest Slingerland catalog, with Gene Krupa on the cover. I recoiled, saying, "What's this? I don't want Slingerland!" Somewhat incredulous, Erwin responded, "But Gene Krupa plays Slingerland." "Yeah," I replied decisively, "but *Ringo* plays Ludwig!" (In all fairness to Slingerland, they made great drums—but it took me another twenty-five years to find that out.)

My parents helped to feed my drum frenzy. My father suffered through my practice sessions, drove me here and there, helped me pack and carry, and never complained. Once my folks took me to the Ludwig factory in Chicago. I was in heaven—but too afraid to go up to God (William F. Ludwig, Sr.). Later we went to visit Rogers. (Boy, did they build great drums. It only took me twenty-one more years to get my first Rogers set.)

Like many players of my generation I played in high school and college, but when it was time to get a "real job," the drums were stacked and stored. Over the next ten years I would fiddle with them or think about fiddling with them. It was about 1980 when I conceived the term "drum malaria." My father had contracted malaria during World War II and there was often talk about how the disease lies dormant in the blood and can reactivate. That is exactly what would happen to me regarding drums. All of a sudden, something would call to me, and the fingers and feet would start moving. Out would come the drums and I would play a bit until the interest was gone. Then I'd put the drums away until the next relapse.

During one of my most feverish outbreaks I decided to invest in a drum shop. I hired two salesmen who worked in a full-line music store that I had started to frequent during one of my drum malaria attacks. I can remember asking them, "Where's Ludwig? Where's Slingerland? Where's Rogers?" What I saw were non-American drums and student-line kits. On the one hand, they told me, that's what most people were buying, and, on the other hand, American quality had slipped. However, if a store would stock professional-quality American products, perhaps….

That simple explanation got me started on the discovery (and re-discovery) process that inspired me to call my friends at *Modern Drummer* and propose this book. In the last six years, I have gladly spent the time and the money necessary to learn about the American drum industry. I have listened to and questioned William F. "Bill" Ludwig, Jr. until we were both worn out. Ben Strauss, of Rogers fame, kindly called and wrote to me on countless occasions. Tom Jenkins of Leedy filled in lots of blanks. The children of U.G. Leedy (Isabelle, Ed, Dorothy, and the late Eugene) visited me—and I peppered them with so many questions that a small family quarrel started. What a host! (Actually, the tough question was, "What kind of car did your dad drive?" The consensus was that it was a LaSalle.)

In 1987, with the help of collectors and dealers who started before me, I began my collection—and my education into the world of American drums. Since I was born in and have lived in Indianapolis for over forty years, I wanted to start my vintage collection with a Leedy snare drum. (Leedy built products in Indianapolis for thirty-five years.) So I bought a Leedy *Elite* snare drum, along with a Rogers *Londoner Five* drumset. I was actually ready to stop there, but about then John Aldridge came into my life. John is the dean of American collectors and the creator/editor of *Not So Modern Drummer,* the official newsletter of people who buy, sell, trade, and cry over the great American drums. John asked me if I was interested in collecting Ludwig tube-lug drums. I told him no—why would anyone want to collect drums from a company still in business? I believed collecting was for the purpose of finding products from the defunct companies, like Leedy. Well, John, of course, was right. I've spent more money on Ludwig drums than on any other brand, and (yes, John) nothing appreciates like an original *Black Beauty.* Since John is ten years younger than I am, I guess I'll sum it up with, "Out of the mouths of babes...."

The American drum industry is over one hundred years old, and this book is really a tribute to the men and women who designed, built, and marketed such great musical instruments. All of us who are involved in drum history are still learning, because so little has been recorded. Catalogs have been around from the beginning, but they tell only part of the story. Our job as collectors and players is to continue to seek out the collectibles, to save them, and to increase the body of information that exists on them.

Vintage drums may never generate the demand—or accrue the value—that vintage guitars bring...but you never know. I've seen the value of some products quadruple in the past five years. Use this book as a guide, whether you are a player looking for a classic sound, a collector who likes to see pretty drums in a case, or an investor looking for a great return. And if you have information that will help our hobby/business, please write to me: Harry Cangany, 10324 Coral Reef Way, Indianapolis, IN 46256.

KEY TO DATA LISTINGS

Each chapter in this book that covers a particular drum manufacturer concludes with a listing of data about the drums that company produced. In order to economize on page space (and eyestrain), the data has been presented in an abbreviated, outline format. That format is structured as follows:

> **Drum Type** (and in some cases Historical Period)
> size(s)
> shell material
> lug description
> strainer description (for snare drums)
> hoop description
> type of plating
> finishes
> additional notes (if applicable)

Owing to the incredible diversity of design and features on the drums made during the period this book covers, not every drum listed will have an entry corresponding to each line above. Some will have fewer line entries, while others will have expanded versions of some of the entries. Once you've looked over a few of the listings and have become familiar with the format, you should be able to easily understand and assimilate the specifications and details presented.

Chapter 1

Camco Drum Company

The Aristocrat of the Drum World

The Camco drum company began life as a machine shop in Oaklawn, Illinois. It gained prominence when its designers created stands that resembled those made by Premier and a pedal modeled after the famous Martin *Fleetfoot*. Camco also made the Gretsch *Floating Action* pedal.

The 1959 Rogers catalog offered Camco products. Today it seems strange to see a competitor giving space and credit to another company, but in 1959 the two were not yet competitors. Camco became a drum manufacturer in 1961 when its president, John Rochon, bought enough George Way Drum Company stock to take control of the business and oust George. (George had established his company in 1954 by purchasing the Elkhart, Indiana factory previously operated by Leedy & Ludwig.) Initially, the company announced that both the Elkhart and Oaklawn locations would be used, but by 1962 all work was moved to Oaklawn, where operations would remain for a decade. Around 1972 Camco was sold to the Kustom Company and moved to Chanute, Kansas. A later sale moved Camco to Los Angeles, where its remnants formed the foundation upon which Drum Workshop is built. (DW purchased the Camco tools and dies in 1979.)

The last Oaklawn Camco drums are identified by an oval white badge; prior to that the winged badge employed by George Way was used. Way's badge was black over brass; Camco's version was white over brass, and that combination remained for the drums built in Kansas and California. Collectors favor the Oaklawn-built drums. It is not uncommon to see Camco shells with missing or incorrect badges.

All Oaklawn Camco shells are coated with white sealer. The California shells were clear-coated at the factory. If you find a clear-coated drum with an Oaklawn badge, one of three things has happened: 1) you have a misbadged drum, 2) someone has removed the white paint, or 3) your drum is not a Camco. Always check the air vent grommet for tampering.

All Camco shells are made from either three or four plies of maple, with reinforcing rings top and bottom. All *Aristocrat* and *Tuxedo* snare models have an extra hole in the shell. Like Gretsch, Camco featured a pop-in drumkey holder—a chromed hex nut with an interior clip to hold the drumkey and prevent it from rattling. This holder was never on the Way models. I mention that in case you find a shell with no identifying badge, but that you can tell takes a Camco lug. A later section of this book will show examples of Camco's lugs, hoops, and strainers.

The Camco hoop, like the Way hoop, is a thing of beauty. Many of us go through the drum world oblivious to the unique designs. While WFL/Ludwig was the originator of the triple-flanged hoop, many companies put their own variations to work. In the case of Camco, the old Leedy hoop—with prominently arched ears—was used. No doubt George Way used the same manufacturer that both Leedy and Leedy & Ludwig had used. Camco, however, had their own rolling machine. It created a high collar with the third flange, and the look was very classy. Because the collar was higher than most other companies' models, players did not get drumkeys stuck during head changes.

In the '60s the emphasis in pro line drums was on pearl or sparkle covered finishes. Camco offered a few wood finishes (and in fact I've found some beautiful shells hidden under plastic coverings), but most of the drums were conventionally covered.

Camco's most unusual finish was called "3-D Moire." Moire was the term Camco used to describe the "satin flame" finish also used by Gretsch and Slingerland. The 3-D was a white, prismatic pattern repeated in rows. Some have described it as hypnotic. Perhaps it was conservative little Camco's attempt to compete with the psychedelic movement then so prevalent in popular culture.

The typical Camco drumset was jazz sized, and most of Camco's national ads featured jazz drummers like Colin Bailey smiling behind a 20/12/14 set in an indeterminate sparkle finish. If you find Camco ads, you'll notice that they are always very small and in black and white. Camco catalogs usually have a color cover shot and then thirty to forty black & white pages. No matter how often the catalogs changed, many of the same pictures were used. In fact, Camco would illustrate holders that they no longer sold or strainers that they no longer made. And if you pay attention, you can see black-badged George Way drums in the pictures long after Camco had taken over.

Quite a few Camco drums came out of the factory without tom or leg holders. Many others were built at the same factory, but with Rogers mounts. Camco's normal single tom holder was a Walberg & Auge model (see chapter 15), but some kind of working relationship with Rogers existed that perhaps went back to the days when Camco pedals and stands were in the Rogers catalog. (Camco's biggest rock artist—Dennis Wilson of the Beach Boys—appeared in photos with a blue moire set with Rogers holders for the tom-tom, cymbal, and floor-tom legs.) Because that relationship existed, I find no problem if a collector has a Camco set with Rogers parts. The originality ends, though, if the drums have been drilled to support something that was not factory authorized. During its heyday, Camco made drums in the following sizes and finishes:

SNARE DRUMS

Aristocrat: (Orchestra)
5x14
8 round lugs
triple-flanged hoops
Aristocrat strainer
pearl, lacquer

(Concert)
6½x14
16 round lugs
triple-flanged hoops
Aristocrat strainer
pearl, lacquer

(Casino)
4½x14
8 round lugs
same as *Orchestra Aristocrat*

(Band)
8x15
16 round lugs
same as *Concert Aristocrat*

Orchestra Tuxedo
5x14, 6½x14
8 *Tuxedo* lugs
triple-flanged hoops
Tuxedo (trapezoid shaped) or
   Aristocrat strainer
pearl, lacquer, metal

Studio
5x14
8 *Tuxedo* lugs
Economy strainer
pearl, lacquer, mahogany, metal

Super
5x14
8 *Tuxedo* lugs
triple-flanged hoops
Parallel strainer
metal

Jazz
3½x14
8 small round lugs
triple-flanged hoops
Economy strainer
pearl, lacquer, mahogany, metal

Early Camco drums featured this winged badge.

Courtesy Rob Cook

From 1962 to 1972 all Camco drums were made in Oaklawn, Illinois, and featured this oval badge.

TOM-TOMS

Aristocrat
8x12, 9x13, 14x14, 16x16

Tuxedo
same sizes
lugs separate-tension but centered on each shell

BASS DRUMS

Aristocrat
14x18, 14x20, 14x22, 14x24

Tuxedo
same sizes but with large *Tuxedo* lugs

Aristocrat and *Tuxedo* model tom-toms and bass drums were available with plastic covering or lacquer finish.

FINISHES

Pearls and sparkles included: black diamond, burgundy, champagne, silver, green, gold, blue, red, jet black, oyster, and white marine. Moires included red, purple, charcoal, aqua, gold and blue, and of course, the famous (or infamous) 3-D.

3-D Moire was Camco's most unusual finish.

Chapter 2

Fibes Drum Corporation

Drivers of Corvettes and Avantis know that fiberglass is a tough and durable product. In 1966, the Fibes concept came about after a few years of tinkering by drummer Bob Grauso and John Morena, a specialist in chemical engineering. The process, or really processes, involved the shaping and stabilizing of the raw material.

Here is a description of the Fibes philosophy:

"The Fibes fiberglass drumshells possess a strength greater than that of steel, and are comparable to or lighter than wood in weight. Their unique process has resulted in such density control as to ensure a consistent tonal response in each and every shell. Also, this controlled alignment of fiberglass permits greater internal vibratory response, thus providing one of the most sensitive and brilliant sounding instruments made today. At the same time, it is a virtually indestructible instrument."

Fibes also built drums called *Crystalites* from acrylics, and a "frosted" version was available. The raised surface resembled frosted glass, and there was a dark tinted version called smoke. Initially laminate covered finishes were available, including chrome, antique copper, antique brass, a wood-grain finish, and black. The strangest options, in my opinion, were the fivels—finishes that resembled velvet in black, peacock or sapphire blue, crimson red, pumpkin orange, or a blending of two or more. (I wonder if anyone ever painted a picture of Elvis on one of these?)

A number of very talented players used Fibes drums, including Alan Dawson, Grady Tate, Lloyd Morales, Arthur Press, Stan Levey, and Jack Sperling. Buddy Rich is famous—or perhaps notorious—for using a

Fibes snare drum while he was an endorser for Rogers and later for Slingerland. Besides the great drum sounds, Fibes also brought us the *Sta-Way* bumper, a product designed to keep tom-toms and snare drums apart. (I once visited the Smithsonian in my capacity as a contributor to *Modern Drummer.* I was allowed into the "inner sanctum" to inspect

Fibes' Crystalite models were among the earliest of the "clear" drums popular in the early 1970s.

Buddy Rich's *Radio King* set, and I noticed that the white marine pearl covering on the 9x13 tom-tom had worn through and that there was damage to the shell. You'd think that Buddy could have gotten a good deal on one of those Fibes *Sta-Way* bumpers.)

Grauso and Morena sold their Farmingdale, New York-based company to the C.F. Martin Organization in 1970. Martin shut down the company and sold it to Jim Corder in 1979. Jim moved the facilities to Huntsville, Alabama, and proceeded to make Corder wood-shell drums using the Fibes lugs, strainers, and hoops. When I asked Jim about his switch to wood, he told me that when he went up to inspect the Fibes factory, he couldn't believe the amount of fiberglass dust. It was everywhere and in everything. He decided then and there that he'd work with wood! Corder later sold the company, which was re-named for its new owner: Sammy Darwin. Darwin, in turn, sold the company again in June 1994. The new owner—Tommy Robertson of Austin, Texas—has returned to the Fibes name. So the look and the heritage of Fibes drums are still with us.

SNARE DRUMS

SFT 690: 5x14, 5½x14, 6x14
triple-flanged hoops
chrome plating

TOM-TOMS

8x12, 9x13, 14x14, 14x16, 16x16, 16x18
triple-flanged hoops
chrome plating

BASS DRUMS

12x18, 12x20, 14x18, 14x20, 14x22, 14x24

FINISHES

listed in text

Chapter 3

Fred Gretsch Manufacturing Company

That Great Gretsch Sound

Gretsch is a company that has enjoyed many lives. From 1883 to 1895, the Brooklyn-based Fred Gretsch Manufacturing Company was owned by Friedrich Gretsch, who had come to America in 1872 and had learned the drum trade in New York City. He died while visiting Germany, and the business went to his teenage son, Fred. *That* Fred has become known as Fred Senior, since *his* son—also named Fred—also figures in the company's history. The Gretsch plant, which became a Brooklyn landmark, handled all sales east of Chicago. The company opened an office in Chicago in 1928—no doubt to compete with the three midwestern firms: Leedy, Ludwig & Ludwig, and Slingerland.

Unlike its Midwest competitors, Gretsch made drums both under their own name and for other firms. I have a 1939 Rogers catalog that quite clearly shows Gretsch drums. My suspicion is that quite a few "trade outs" existed. Gretsch got wheeled consoles (the forerunners of today's drum racks) and strainers from Premier, and three-point strainers from Slingerland. Gretsch sent shells to Rogers and probably got calf heads in return.

By the 1930s, the Gretsch name was a serious contender in the marketplace. Jo Jones, drummer with the Count Basie band, was an early and prominent endorser. Jo had one of the first tunable tom-tom sets. The drums had timpani handles (T-rods) instead of drum rods to tighten the heads. (I wonder how often his sticks got caught on those T's?) Another Gretsch endorser was the amazing Chick Webb. Chick was an incredibly talented player who—despite being deformed by tuberculosis of the spine—outplayed anybody in his path. Chick played a custom Gretsch set on a Premier wheeled console. The drums were known as Gretsch-Gladstones.

Billy Gladstone was a famous New York City theater drummer. He was featured at the Capitol Theatre and later at Radio City Music Hall. Besides being a consummate artist, Gladstone was also an inventor. Among many other innovations, Billy invented a tuning process to help theater drummers who sat in damp orchestra pits. His snare drums had either three- or two-way tuning. A special key had either three or two openings. In the three-way, the position of the key

allowed tensioning of just the batter head, just the snare head, or both—all accomplished without lifting the drum. Gretsch made the Gretsch-Gladstone drums. (See Chapter 18: Most Collectible Snare Drums.) Years later, Billy bought shells from Gretsch to make his own Billy Gladstone drums. (See Chapter 16: Honorable Mention.)

The Jo Jones, Chick Webb, and Billy Gladstone situations point out the power that Gretsch had in its home town. That power was put on hold during the war years. But after World War II, Fred Gretsch, Jr.—who returned to take the presidency of the company—met with his executives and decided to develop the brand into one of truly national importance.

In the late 1940s and early '50s a trend started. Drummers wanted smaller drums. I'm told that this came about because professionals in cities like New York had to jam their gear in cabs. Former Benny Goodman drummer Dave Tough (who

In 1941 the Gretsch factory in Brooklyn was a landmark
in the drumming industry.

used Gretsch drums between stints with Slingerland and WFL) got to know the Gretsch management because Goodman had a contract with Gretsch. Tough has been given credit for urging the development of the 20" bass drum with disappearing spurs and cymbal holder. The catalogs of the '50s and '60s are loaded with endorsers: Mel Lewis, Max Roach, Art Blakey, Chico Hamilton, Elvin Jones, Don Lamond, and one of my favorites, the powerful and flamboyant Sonny Payne (who inherited and redefined the drum sound in the Basie Band). Louie Bellson—probably the nicest man ever to pick up drumsticks—created his signature look with Gretsch. Louie went to Gretsch in 1947 with an idea for a double-bass kit that included an enormous tom-tom—really a cocktail size—between the two bass drums. He has written that other companies laughed at his idea, but Gretsch came through.

I wrote once that no other company seems to enjoy the brand loyalty that Gretsch does. Lots of endorsers for other manufacturers quietly talk about the little round-badge Gretsch kit they still have at home in the closet or down at the studio. There's also the lament of the set that got sold for one pitiful reason or another. Finding another Gretsch set is often a quest.

The Gretsch logo was stamped on a round badge through the time period selected for this book. But the drums of note are really Gretsch-Gladstones of the late '30s and early '40s and the Gretsch drums and sets of the '50s and '60s. Again, this mirrors the philosophy of Gretsch. Until World War II the emphasis was to build drums for other people. From the late '40s on, it was to bring Gretsch into the national spotlight.

In the early '50s, the shells were three plies of maple. Initially the interiors of the shells were clear-coated; later they were covered in a silver paint. Here's a tidbit: One of the causes of the "Great Gretsch Sound" may be linen! Under the plastic covering of the '50s drums was a cloth wrap. (And you thought it was the silver paint!) By the '60s, the number of plies grew to six.

Early rockers favored Gretsch—D.J. Fontana with Elvis, for example. But when Ringo Starr hit these shores, Gretsch was unprepared. The company was jazz-oriented and as a result was passed over by rock players of the '60s in favor of Ludwig and Rogers.

In 1967, Fred Gretsch, Jr. surprised his staff by announcing his decision to sell the company to the Baldwin Piano Company. (This was at around the same time CBS bought Rogers and Fender and when Camco was talking to Kustom.) Baldwin moved the factory to Arkansas, where it stayed until it was purchased in 1983 by yet another Fred Gretsch (III) and re-located to South Carolina.

During each move, the Gretsch badge design was changed. Collectors know to play safe and stick to the Brooklyn round badge. Don't be surprised to find round-badge tom-toms without air vents. Many of them have badges that are tacked on using decorative upholstery tacks.

Gretsch called their lugs *Broadkasters*. The first version was an art deco model with a diamond pattern. (Some people refer to them as the "Rocket" lugs.) These lugs touched the shells in two places (at the screw holes); the middle of the lug was cut away. Looking at the lug from its side, one would say it resembled a backward "C." The modern Gretsch lug was introduced in the 1950s. It was also called the *Broadkaster* initially; later it was referred to simply as the "drum rod casing."

Gretsch also sold a very popular pedal known as the *Floating Action* model. It was actually designed and built by Camco (when it was known as the Camco Drum Accessory Company) and was almost identical to that company's own pedal. The only difference was the design of the footboard. Gretsch was also the original importer of Turkish K Zildjian cymbals, so you may find a drumset equipped with them. Typically, collectors discover Constantinople Ks with 1950s-era sets and Istanbul Ks with drums from the '60s.

SNARE DRUMS

Gretsch-Gladstone
$6\frac{1}{2}$x14 (special sizes possible)
8 tube lugs—special threading
die-cast hoops
chrome plating
Gladstone strainer

Broadkaster Name Band
5x14, $5\frac{1}{2}$x14, $6\frac{1}{2}$x14
wood shell ('40s through '60s)
metal shell ('40s)
8 *Broadkaster* lugs (two versions)
die-cast hoops (double-flanged through 1950s)
Radio King strainer (1940s)
Micro-Sensitive strainer (1950-60s)
pearl, lacquer, mahogany

Broadkaster Floor Show
$6\frac{1}{2}$x14
same as '50s and '60s *Name Band* but with 16 separate
    small tom-tom lugs

Renown
5x14, $5\frac{1}{2}$x14, $6\frac{1}{2}$x14
8 *Broadkaster* lugs
single-flanged hoops with clips
small snare strainer (*Premier*) (1940s)
Renown strainer (1950s-1960)
lacquer, mahogany

Economy
5x14, $5\frac{1}{2}$x14, $6\frac{1}{2}$x14
1940s—brass or wood 6 lug
1950s-60s—wood shell only and called *The Dixieland*
nickel plating in the '40s
chrome plating in the '50s and '60s
lacquer, mahogany

Broadkaster Max Roach
1950s—8 small *Broadkaster* lugs
die-cast hoops
nickel or chrome plating

Louie Bellson on his unique Gretsch kit, circa 1947

Progressive Jazz
chrome plating
1960s—*Micro-Sensitive* strainer
usually pearl

Metal Snare
1960s—5x14
8 *Broadkaster* lugs
die-cast hoops
Micro-Sensitive strainer

Broadkaster Concert
7x14, 8x15
same as the *Floor Show*, but deeper

Gretsch also built a number of junior drums—single-tension metal and wood shells in the following sizes: $3\frac{1}{2}$x13, 4x13, and 5x14. Each used the most rudimentary strainer.

In the '40s, Gretsch also experimented with *Catalina* snares, basses, and toms. These were moderately priced wood shells in lacquer with plastic lugs, small *Premier* strainers, and single-flanged hoops.

TOM-TOMS
8x12, 9x13, 14x14, 16x16, 16x18
note: the 8x12 and 9x13 had 10 lugs (5 per head) instead of 12 as with every other company
Broadkaster lugs
die-cast hoops
pearl, lacquer

BASS DRUMS
Broadkaster Dance
14x18, 14x20, 14x22, 14x24
Broadkaster lugs
pearl covered only

Concert
14x26, 14x28, 16x30, 16x32
pearl, lacquer, mahogany

Single Tension Concert
14x24, 14x26, 14x28, 16x30, 16x32
lug casing to receive long T-rod that tightened into threaded claw
pearl, lacquer, mahogany

Renown
14x22, 14x24, 14x26, 14x28
center support to receive long T-rod that tightened into threaded claw
mahogany, solid or tri-tone lacquer

Special notes on Gretsch: Many of the snare drums in the '60s have the special and exclusive wide-band "power snares." These were 42-strand snares standard on the *Name Band*, the *Floor Show*, the *Progressive Jazz*, and the *Metal Snare Drum*.

FINISHES
1930s-40s
white oriental (marine) pearl, smoke oriental (black diamond) pearl, gold sparkle, silver sparkle, green sparkle, blue sparkle, duco (lacquer), blue and silver, blue and gold, red and gold, black and gold, red and silver

1950s add
peacock sparkle, red sparkle, midnight blue, cameo coral, cadillac green, copper mist, diamond sparkle, jet black

1960s add
champagne sparkle, tangerine sparkle, burgundy sparkle, starlight sparkle, emerald green pearl, red wine pearl, aqua flame, gold flame, moonglow flame, peacock flame, chrome nitron, gold nitron

A 1950s-era kit in blue sparkle

Chapter 4

Leedy Manufacturing Company

World's Finest Drummers' Instruments

In 1895, a young man named Ulysses Grant Leedy from Fostoria, Ohio joined a clarinet player named Sam Cooley to manufacture drums in Indianapolis, Indiana. Leedy came to his adopted city to play with the orchestra of the English Opera House (the leading theater for opera and the legitimate stage in Indianapolis).

Leedy had two advantages when it came to making drums: time and mechanical ability. His father was a cabinet maker, so the necessary woodworking skills came naturally to young U.G. His products became so popular that two Chicago players (who were also brothers) became Leedy dealers. Their last name was Ludwig.

U.G. put together four factories during his life. The first Leedy location was in a round building two blocks from the center of downtown Indianapolis. It was known as the Cyclorama Building and originally featured large, circular paintings of the Battle of Gettysburg. Its advantage to Leedy was that it was very close to the English Theater—close enough, in fact, for "Lys" to run to his next performance in between manufacturing steps.

The story of Leedy (Indianapolis) is the story of U.G. Leedy. Sure there were lots of employees—key people like George Way, Herman Winterhoff, Alfred Kuerst, and others. But the main player was always Ulysses Grant Leedy. As a youngster, he had played in Cedar Point, Ohio with the Great Western Band. He then went on the road for several years until he came to Indianapolis. He spent ten years at the English until he left to become a full-time manufacturer.

During his time on the road, Leedy made drums for himself and other players. In 1903, he left the Cyclorama Building to establish the first part of the great Leedy factory at Palmer and Barth streets. By 1919, he had sixty employees. Most of them, according to *Indiana And Indianans,* were "skilled specialists, who received their training directly from Mr. Leedy himself."

One of the factory's greatest achievements came in 1919, when they were able to fulfill an order from Purdue University to build the world's largest bass drum. Imagine the problem: The company could not decide on the dimensions of the drum until the two largest calf heads in history were processed! Leedy wrote: "After an extended search two bull hides were obtained that permitted us to make a drum shell that would measure seven feet in diameter." (The finished drum actually measured 7'3" in diameter by 45" deep!)

U.G. Leedy favored solid-shell wooden snare drums, and he personally designed and built a machine to heat and bend the wood to make them. Eventually he also built snare drums from brass. But this happened only after his Chicago dealer,

U.G. Leedy (bottom row, fifth from left) with members of his staff, in the early 1920s

Ludwig & Ludwig, became a competitor—which is a story worthy of a brief digression.

William F. Ludwig, Sr. once played a snare-drum duet with Tom Mills, a man who was referred to as "Sousa's favorite drummer." The unnamed wood-shell snare used by Ludwig was no match for the crisp, ringing sound coming from the 6½x13 German-made brass snare drum played by Mills. Ludwig was so enamored of the drum that he had to have it, and a few years later (so the story goes) he was able to buy the drum by redeeming a pawn ticket.

Ludwig took the drum to Indianapolis to convince U.G. Leedy to build one like it. Leedy refused because he thought walnut and maple were the only raw materials that should be used to make snare drums. It may have been a bad judgment call on U.G.'s part, because Ludwig returned to Chicago, copied the Mills drum himself, put a Ludwig & Ludwig badge on it (see the chapters on Ludwig & Ludwig, WFL, and the Ludwig Drum Company), and went into the manufacturing business himself.

In 1919 Leedy made the "world's largest bass drum" for Purdue University. U.G. is at the center (in the striped tie); a young Cecil Strupe is on his right.

While the matter of the Mills drum may have been a mistake on U.G. Leedy's part, he still did a lot of things that turned out favorably. For instance, he designed the first snare drum stand. He also made his metal shells from one piece of spun brass. And the first practical semi-self-aligning lug came from his factory—as did the floating head concept. (In this idea, the counterhoop comes down over the flesh hoop, and rods pass through it. Today we'd call this idea a double-flanged hoop.) In addition, the first pearl coverings—known as *Pyralins*—came out on Leedy drums. And Leedy built the first vibraphone—in fact, he was marvelously successful with all mallet instruments.

One cannot help but be struck by the quality of Leedy work. The designs, the machining, and the woodwork are all top-notch.

In fact, the only weakness of Leedy drums was their strainers. Most were designed by Cecil Strupe (who went on to work for L&S and very early WFL). In each case, his toggle throwoffs were fragile to the touch. The first mass-produced strainer—the *Utility*—was used through 1949. It was simple, easy, and dependable. But it was also homely, and the farther one got from its patent date of 1911, the homelier it got. Leedy was forced to compete head-on with Ludwig & Ludwig, the company that made the best strainers in the business. Leedy's *Presto, Marvel,* and *Speedway* strainers were accidents ready to happen. But everything else on Leedy products was among the finest designed and built on earth.

Leedy Manufacturing continued to grow. By 1923, sales manager George Way had been in his job for two years. At that point he launched *Leedy Drum Topics,* an eight-page black & white quarterly newsletter. In each of the twenty-nine issues published, Way was able to showcase products, endorsers, regional players, and readers' suggestions—along with sales pitches and whimsy.

The late '20s were a wonderful time for the company: The factory grew, and Leedy products became more modern and were shipped all over the world. But U.G. Leedy was a sick man; he had developed heart disease. His wife Zoa was quite a bit younger, and their four children had college to complete. U.G. came to the conclusion that the best protection for his family would be to sell the company. So, in 1929, U.G. signed a contract to sell his thirty-four-year-old company to C.G. Conn, Ltd., the giant band-instrument manufacturer, for $950,000 in cash.

Within a month, the stock market fell. And while U.G. and Zoa were on an extended vacation, Conn's president, C.D. Greenleaf, gave the order to move the factory to Elkhart. That decision stranded many Leedy workers who didn't want to leave Indianapolis. U.G. came back to town and promised these loyal workers that they would have jobs. He bought a building and began to set up the last of his factories: Leedy & Sons. But more on that in another chapter. For now, we celebrate the drums of Leedy Manufacturing, whose motto was always "World's Finest Drummers' Instruments."

The most collectible Leedy drums are the *Black Elite,* the *Marvel,* and any of the floating-head drums, either wood or metal. These drums are all from the 1920s. Earlier drums were thumbscrew models and deserve our attention, but typically are not sought-after because they predate lugs. About 1920, the *Multi* model was produced—so we'll use that as the logical point to start collecting. There is one early drum, however, that would be worth a small fortune if it could be found.

I have an undated catalog that lists the Leedy address as rooms 14, 16, and 18 in the Cyclorama Building. Someone, using ink, has crossed out the address and written in "1063 E. Palmer Street." So the catalog must be from 1903 at the latest—and I suspect it's the oldest Leedy catalog in existence. In its tiny pages, U.G. Leedy illustrated his products. One of them defies description. It is *the* drum to find: "A 6x15 second-growth walnut [snare] drum, beautifully hand-carved and fitted with oxidized copper rods and trimmings." The catalog goes on to say that this kind of drum was "special fine...for presentation purposes." Today we would give an exceptional drummer a trophy or a plaque. Ninety years ago such a drummer would receive a work of art.

SNARE DRUMS 1920-1929
Multi-model
4x14, 5x14, 6x14, 7x14, 8x14, 9x14,
10x14, 12x14, 4x15, 5x15, 6x15, 7x15,
8x15, 9x15, 10x15, 12x15
walnut, maple, mahogany, or double-
   inverted-bead brass shell
8 flat slotted fillister-head screw rods,
   or square-head screw key rods,
   or thumb screw rods
Utility strainer
double-channel counterhoops
originally nickel (satin finish) or
   natural wood finish, then white or
   black enamel or nobby gold on shell
   or just hoops, rods, and strainers.
   (See the Glossary.)
Also available in genuine gold plate.
Engraving offered by 1924.

U.G. Leedy designed these bending machines to create solid-wood drumshells.

Utility
4x14, 5x14, 6x14, 7x14, 4x15, 5x15, 6x15, 7x15
solid-wood or double-inverted-bead brass shell
   (plated in nickel)
flat hoops with clips
initially 8 lugs

By 1925, Leedy introduced lugs attached by four small
   screws. Previously two larger screws held a similar
   lug in place.

Professional: (Floating Head)
solid-walnut or double-inverted-bead brass shell
   (nickel-plated)
8 lug
key rods
double-flanged hoops
Presto strainer

Elite: (Black Elite)
4x14, 5x14, 6x14
same as metal-shell *Professional* but plated in black nickel,
   engraved to show a design in the brass
hoops, rods, strainer, and butt plate finished in nobby gold

FINISHES
Utility, Professional, Elite:
wood shells: black or white enamel
metal shells: white enamel, nobby gold, or real gold
hoops and hardware: nickel, nobby gold, or real gold

Reliance (1925)
4x14, 5x14, 6x14
one-piece metal shells or solid wood
6 tube lugs
flat hoops with clips
Utility strainernickel or mahogany

In 1926, the *Pyralins* were introduced. White marine and
sparkling gold were the first two, followed by black onyx, red
onyx, rainbow, green pearl, and black (diamond) pearl. Also
available were Tudor (polished mahogany) and gold, black,
red, or white duco. Duco was enamel at Leedy
(Indianapolis). Later, Leedy (Elkhart) and Leedy & Ludwig
used lacquer.

1926 also saw the introduction of the *Speedway* strainer—really a *Presto* with a side extension arm raised or lowered into position and tightened with a knob at the bottom of
the arm. In the 1925 "N" catalog, Leedy introduced the
Marvel—another *Presto* variation that was offered for one

year. With the *Marvel,* a *Floating Head* drum would have
snares constantly under tension and raised or lowered on a
"bridge" similar to the Rogers *Dyna-Sonic* principle introduced thirty-seven years later.

BASS DRUMS
1920-1924
Standard
10 to 16x24, 10 to 18x26, 12 to 18x28, 12 to 18x30,
12 to 18x32, 14 to 18x34, 14 to 22x36, 16 to 22x40
solid mahogany or maple with reinforcement hoops
center support held on with two screws from the outside
thumb rods
maple counterhoops

Economy
(later Special)
12 sizes
solid maple
single-tension thumb rods
ebony hoops

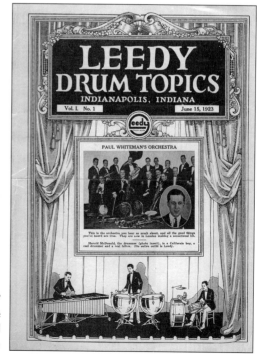

"Leedy Drum Topics"
was perhaps the
earliest drum-related
magazine.

1924 on

12 sizes
mahogany shell
add separate-tension bass drum tube lugs
   with thumb rods

At this point, Leedy experimented with a synthetic (plastic) shell called *Vultex*, which was finished to look like mahogany. Leedy made snares and bass drums of the material.

TOM-TOMS

1920-1924
Chinese

first 6" and 9" diameter, later add 10", 12", and 15" diameters

Tom A Phones

4 (10", 12", 14," 16") with turning handles

by 1925

Standard's center support became a stud
   (like Ludwig & Ludwig's)

add Reliance

2-ply laminated shell of mahogany with maple counterhoops
available with:
   1) thumb rods without center supports
   2) thumb rods with center supports
   3) timpani rods with center supports

by 1927

9x13, 12x14, 16x16
solid or laminated shell
non-tunable drums used tacked heads
tunable drums were either single-tension
   or used tube lugs and timpani rods
special tunable drums in 12" diameter (4 rods) and
   14" diameter (6 rods) resembled modern RotoToms
   in depth

by 1929

All metal work in either chrome, nickel, nobby gold,
   or real gold

This illustration from Leedy's 1903 catalog depicts their exquisite Presentation drum.

Chapter 5

Leedy — Elkhart

C.D. Greenleaf, president of C.G. Conn Ltd., personally negotiated with U.G. Leedy to buy Leedy Manufacturing in October 1929. (See the previous chapter.) Although he had originally agreed to keep the Indianapolis factory open, in the spring of 1930 C.D. told sales manager George Way to head 'em up and move 'em out to Elkhart, 130 miles to the north. The new home for the Leedy factory was christened the "Leedy Building," but was also still called by its original name, the Buescher Building. It was located at 225 East Jackson Street until it was demolished in 1993.

The Conn-owned Leedy company released a four-page flyer to coincide with the move. It featured George Way and mixed cartoon-like drawings and photographs to partially explain the new address. What was stated was that Leedy had made a "progressive move" to the band-instrument capital of the world. The factory was pictured—but not to scale; it looks the size of ten football fields. The ad copy that Way approved (and probably wrote) told readers that Elkhart was a railroad terminal and an air and bus stop. The Great Lakes were close for shipping, and the Mississippi and Ohio Rivers weren't far away. The steel of Chicago and northwest Indiana was even closer. The brass of Wisconsin and the hides and lumber from Illinois were just around the corner. That was all true, but it was only a half-truth. Nowhere was there any message about a change in ownership or the absence of former "movers and shakers" U.G. Leedy, Cecil Strupe, and Herman Winterhoff.

The Leedy "S" catalog came out in 1930 and featured a newly designed line of drums. The funny thing is that the catalog is imprinted with the Indianapolis address, and there is a stamped message on the front cover that reads "Leedy Mfg. Co., Elkhart, Indiana." This, I think, bears witness to Ed Leedy's memory of his father's surprise at learning of the Conn decision to move the factory.

In 1925, Leedy (Indianapolis) had started using a logo that featured a stylized script of the name with a large "L." Until the move to the Elkhart location, there were no badges—just vent holes and engraved hoops and strainer knobs. By 1930, the hoops read "Leedy Elkhart, U.S.A." Shortly after, a customized rectangular badge with raised areas in the middle of the top and bottom was unveiled. This decision was retained through 1949 with only one change: the style of the script of the word "Leedy." In 1950, Conn merged the Leedy and Ludwig companies, and a new and very distinctive badge was created. (More on that in the Leedy & Ludwig chapter.)

Throughout the '30s and '40s, Leedy represented American craftsmanship at its best. Hopefully, you will have a chance to inspect a Leedy shell and see the wonderful work. In 1930, the company released the first *Broadway* series—the high-end snare drums named by George Way. Way, the traveler, loved New York City and likened the drums to great performers awash in bright lights and excitement. With the release of the initial *Broadway* series, Leedy presented the first truly mod-

This '30s-era Leedy Broadway snare featured the first truly modern tuning lug, which has come to be known as the "X-lug."

ern lug: the X lug (sometimes called the Box lug). Leedy didn't *call* it the X lug, but we do because of the design of an X on the front of each lug. Prior to the X, Leedy drums were fitted with lugs held in place by four external screws. Right before that, a similar lug had two mounting screws and a slightly different look. The X lugs were created by Cecil Strupe. The big nuts did not fully swivel, so I call them "semi-self-aligning" lugs.

The 1930 look was probably the last design personally approved by U.G. Leedy, and the emphasis was clearly on the emergence of parallel strainers. The influence of Ludwig & Ludwig on Leedy was clear. Of course, the reverse was also true. The irony of the situation is that these two superpowers were about to become allies.

From 1930 to 1938, the X lug was used on high-end snares, while tube lugs were used on lower-cost models. Tom-toms in this time period came in three variations: tacked heads, early tunable, and X-lug fully tunable. Any time a tacked head was called for, companies used pigskin. The fatty content of pigskin (as opposed to calfskin) kept the thick, stretched look needed for non-tunable drums. The first tunable toms had small lugs and timpani rods on the tops and tacked heads on the bottoms. These small lugs were not X lugs but a separate design. Finally, following Slingerland's lead, Leedy unveiled a fully tunable tom-tom in 1938.

The next major design introduction was the second series *Broadway,* which came out in 1933-36. The *Broadway Standard Strainer* replaced the *Speedway* (a holdover from the '20s). New parallel and dual-strainer systems were revealed. These clearly resembled the Ludwig & Ludwig units. By 1939, the third series of *Broadways* was ready to be shipped. These drums featured either the new *Standard* strainer—a three-hole model that Slingerland continued making through the '60s—or the final parallel design. The dual system was dropped because of low sales; the parallel disappeared with the World War II slowdown.

In late 1938, Leedy introduced its final lug design: the *Beavertail.* Built in three sizes (snare, small tom, and large tom/bass), the *Beavertail* had a simple but graceful design and was used through the Slingerland years to about 1970. By the time of the introduction of the *Beavertails,* Leedy changed direction and made all drums from plies of wood. Gone were the solid-shell *Broadways.* I have heard that a few post-1939 solid-shell *Broadways* exist, but these are probably the result of finished shells sitting around and finally being used.

During the war years, Leedy maintained some sense of normalcy by building the *Dreadnaughts.* These were wooden drums with hand-carved wooden lugs and hoops. To keep metal usage down for the vital war effort, only the rods, strainers, and butt plate were metal.

By 1938 Leedy had introduced drums with the Beavertail lug—a design that lasted until 1970.

After the war, Leedy geared up for peacetime production by issuing a new price list for the 1941-42 catalog items. The *Broadway Standard* became the lead model and was officially called the *Broadway,* since there were no sister models requiring differentiation.

In 1949, Leedy produced an updated logo showing a less stylized version of the name. But in 1950, it was time to change everything again. The Conn organization decided it would be cost-effective to merge their two brands into one company. (Besides Leedy, Conn had also purchased Ludwig & Ludwig in 1930. (See chapter 10 for details.) This led to the creation of Leedy & Ludwig. (See chapter 7.) Of course, a purist might point out that the two brands had been effectively merged since 1930, considering that the drums of both companies were made in the same Elkhart factory and were essentially identical. But the merger technically took place in 1950.

The management of the newly combined companies was moved from the Leedy Building to the Conn Administration Building, but the factory was left unchanged. There was great discomfort, however, among the employees of the two lines—even though the brands had been built side-by-side for twenty years. Dealers were even more upset, because in most cities Leedy and Ludwig & Ludwig had separate franchises. As the lines were merged, Conn had to cut dealers, which did not play well.

To summarize the history of Leedy drums (other than the brief period when drums with the Leedy name were made by Slingerland, as outlined in the next chapter), we can say that they were the industry leaders up until the 1920s. At that point their preeminence was challenged by Bill Ludwig, Sr., to a point where the Leedy and Ludwig & Ludwig lines were equals. By 1930 both lines had been sold to Conn, and Slingerland started to come on strong—itself taking preeminence during the '30s, largely based on its endorsers. Although Leedy quality did not suffer as a result of the move to Elkhart, the drums were looked at as "old-fashioned" compared to Slingerland's *Radio Kings.* I believe that if one dispassionately examines the finished products in terms of woodworking, metalcraft, etc., it's evident that Leedy drums were better-built. But passion had (and still has) a lot to do with drumming. Krupa reigned in the '30s, and his bombastic style and showmanship sold a lot of drums for H.H. Slingerland.

However, drummers today are rediscovering the value and quality of Leedy drums. Although the Leedy Manufacturing Company has been gone for over forty years, it seems that every week more collectors are enchanted with the wonderful products made in Indianapolis and Elkhart.

SNARE DRUMS

Broadway Dual
first series *Dual* 1930-1932
second series *Dual* 1933-1936 (model ends)

Broadway Parallel
first series *Parallel* 1930-1932
second series *Parallel* 1933-1937
third series *Parallel* 1937-1946 (model ends)

Broadway Standard
first series *Standard: Speedway* strainer 1930-1936
second series *Standard* 1936-1940
third series *Standard* 1941-1949
5x14
solid mahogany shell (through '30s), then laminated
6½x14
metal
6½x15
nickel, chrome, or nobby gold
7x14 (by '42)
8x15 (by '41)
8x14 (by '42)
8 X lugs (*Beavertails* by 1938-39)
double-flanged hoops

Elite
same sizes as *Broadways*
black nickel or white enamel (*Black Elite* is engraved)
chrome or nobby gold plating

Reliance
(later the *Utility*)
4x14, 5x14, 6½x14 by 1940
metal or solid mahogany (through the '30s), then laminated
6 tube lugs (*Reliance* becomes 8 lugs in 1933 and *Presto*
  strainer gets 4 screw holes. *Beavertails* by 1949.)
flat hoops, clips
Presto strainer

Standard Orchestra
4x14, 5x14, 6½x15
solid walnut
14 thumb rods
maple hoops
Presto strainer
gone by 1932

Tango model
4x14
solid mahogany
8 thumb rods
flat hoops with clips
Utility strainer

Pep model
4x14
3-ply mahogany
6 thumb rods
flat hoops
Nifty strainer
by 1934, used Ludwig *Universal* strainer

Nifty model
3x13
same as the *Pep*
by 1934, used a Ludwig *Universal* strainer and was
  also available with metal shell

Broadway Swingster (1937)
7x14, 8x14
solid mahogany shell
8 X lugs (16 *Beavertails* by 1939)
wooden counterhoops with claws, or double-flanged
  counterhoops
nickel or chrome plating
third series *Parallel* or second and third series *Standard* strainer

Broadway Concert King (1938)
8x15
same features as *Swingster* with double-flanged
  counterhoops

Commander
8x15
3-ply mahogany
16 pressed steel lugs
single-flanged hoops with clips
Presto strainer
black or white lacquer

Challenger (1942)
6½x14
16 *Beavertail* lugs
single-flanged hoops with clips
Presto strainer
marine green pearl or lacquer

During World War II, the *Commander* and the *Victory* were
the names used for the *Reliance* and *Utility*. Pressed steel
lugs were used instead of tube lugs.

BASS DRUMS

14x26
(by 1938)
12x16
14x28
solid mahogany (*Standard*) through 1930s
16x30
16x32
3-ply mahogany (*Spartan*)
16x34
16x36
tube lugs (single- or separate-tension) initially,
  chrome, nickel, or nobby gold *Beavertail* lugs by 1938,
  half-moon lugs on single-tension

FINISHES
(for snares and above-listed bass drums)
marine pearl, gold sparkle, silver sparkle, red sparkle, green
pearl, black (diamond), black onyx, rainbow, oriental pearl,
black (nickel for snare drums), autographs of the stars, black
and gold, cream and gold, marine green, maroon and gold,
black enamel (bass drums), white enamel, mahogany. (Non-
standard finishes available: red, orange, yellow, blue with
choice color on hoops and another on shell and hoops. By
1934, blue and silver lacquer.)

8x24
2 ply mahogany (*Reliance*)
12x24
12x26
separate-tension
14x28
single-tension with center support
14x30
single-tension without center support
16x30

by 1949
Broadway bass drums were also available in: 14x20, 14x22, 14x24.

TOM-TOMS

pre-1933
4x10, 9x13, 12x14, 16x16
pigskin heads, both heads tacked

by 1933
tunable toms with timpani rods on top and tacked bottom
  heads
rods tighten into very small lugs resembling upside-down
  chevrons
nickel, chromium, nobby gold plating
same finishes as with snare drums
heads are pigskin

by 1937
same sizes
separate-tension tunable toms with rods on both sides
small chevron lugs
nobby gold not available

by 1938
7x11, 8x12, 9x13, 12x14, 14x16
separate-tension X lugs, immediately followed by
  Beavertails
single-flanged hoops and clips
key rods
nickel or chrome plating
pearl or lacquer
16x16 ('42)
18x20 ('49)
20x20 ('49)

Single-headed tom-toms were introduced in two sizes: 7x10
and 9x13, available in cream, gold, and nickel.

This spread in Leedy's 1945 catalog highlights the company's 50th anniversary, and illustrates the diversity of products it offered.

Chapter 6

Leedy — Chicago

Superior Drummers' Instruments Since 1894

H. "Bud" Slingerland, Jr. was the undisputed king of his company, and he took great delight in tweaking the corporate nose of WFL/Ludwig. There are stories of Bud and Bill Ludwig, Jr. competing for the same timpani orders and fighting for the same endorsers. Both companies battled in court over the design of the hoops holding plastic heads. But there are a few instances of cooperation between the two. For example, Bill Ludwig, Jr. remembers sharing pearl covering with Bud when Slingerland ran low. But in 1955 the "boys" cooperated on something major.

Discussed in detail in other chapters of this book are the reasons Conn had for the dissolution of Leedy & Ludwig. Bill Ludwig, Jr. and WFL came forward with $90,000 to buy the Ludwig & Ludwig name, tools, dies, and patents. He also talked Bud Slingerland into buying Leedy from Conn for the same amount.

Every time I think about the Slingerland move, I am astounded. What did they have to gain? Leedy & Ludwig had been inactive for a model year—and buyers had gone to Slingerland, WFL, Gretsch, and Rogers anyway. Bud's theory was that he could create a second dealer network. The best stores in each town would carry Slingerland, and he would give the Leedy line to the second-best store. (Those were the days when drum lines were sacred and a dealer represented only one.) His thrust was against WFL and the Ludwigs, yet his move only made them stronger. They solidified the WFL and Ludwig & Ludwig brand names into one, and the 1956 Ludwig Drum Company became as strong as WFL had been—and much stronger than Ludwig & Ludwig.

The Chicago Slingerland factory became the manufacturer of Leedy drums. The earliest models are identified by a brass oval; later models featured a blue oval badge—the same physical size as the black oval Slingerland badge. The drums *looked* like Leedy, but they were clearly

Slingerland mahogany shells with a mix of Slingerland and Leedy hardware. Let's go drum by drum.

On the bass drums, the claws were the same design for both companies. The marching drums actually used the old Ludwig & Ludwig-style claws. The T-rods were old-style Slingerland. The hoops had ½" inlays, just like Slingerland's. (Leedy used ¾" strips of pearl.) The lugs were Leedy.

The tom-toms used Leedy lugs, but the hoops were Slingerland *Stick Savers*. The tone control and the legs and brackets were also Slingerland. The tom holder was the Walberg & Auge model used by Slingerland, and featured a diamond plate on the ride tom. The double holder was clearly the early Slingerland double-ratchet model.

Slingerland hoops were present on the snare drums other than the non-professional models (the *Reliance* and *Utility*, which used single-flanged and straight hoops, respectively). The *Shelly Manne* model (the 5½x14 *Broadway*, really) and the regular 6½ and 8x14 *Broadway* used the reliable Leedy *Broadway* strainer introduced in the late '30s–but with

This brass oval badge identifies Leedy drums made in Chicago under Slingerland's ownership in the mid-1950s. Later models featured a blue oval badge.

Slingerland *Radio King* snares. The other Chicago Leedy snare drums used either the *Krupa Radio King* strainer or the *Rapid*. The *Krupa* was called the *Professional* strainer and the *Rapid* was referred to as the *Instant Throwoff* in the Leedy catalog. Each snare drum used a Slingerland muffler.

The post-1955 Leedy catalogs are far cries from the works of art put forward by George Way in Leedy's earlier heyday. They are thirty-five pages, with nothing to spare. Many of the illustrations are clearly Leedy & Ludwig pictures with the distinctive badge showing.

The stands and spurs are definitely Slingerland. The only new item was a snare casing built to resemble two *Beavertail* lugs backed into one another. Leedy Elkhart never got around to building a center-mounted separate-tension lug for snare drums. *Broadways* were deep enough to use two rows of small *Beavertails*. The 4x14 *Broadway New Era* had side-to-side *Beavertails*. But when 4½", 5", and 5½" drums were requested, Slingerland decided to use a new lug. They did, however, like the design of the *Broadway* buttplate, so they placed it also on their *Artist* model drums. The *Artist* used the *Radio King* shell with a *Zoomatic* strainer and extension snares. The *Zoomatic* replaced the "clamshell" (*Super* strainer).

I'm told that Bud Slingerland had a second reason for buying Leedy, which was to get his hands on timpani designs that went back to the days of U.G. Leedy. But no matter how many reasons he had to make the purchase, it looks like he needed only one to shut the operation down. That reason was that Chicago Leedy was a flop. Although the company had big-name endorsers (like Shelly Manne, Jack Sperling, and Roy Harte) and funds were spent in advertising, the buying public wasn't there. The "real" Leedy was gone, and the "real" Slingerland was alive and well. There was no great need for a mix of the two.

Don't misunderstand my viewpoint. There are beautiful Chicago Leedy drums that sound as good today as the day they were made. But the operation of Leedy by Slingerland was an exercise that was probably doomed from the beginning. It was a sad ending to the story of a former champion. But who knows, maybe someday Leedy will live again.

If you find a shell with Leedy lugs and no badge or hoops to identify the era of manufacture, or if you find a drum with Slingerland hoops but no badge, just look at the interior. Elkhart Leedys and Leedy & Ludwig drums have a clear or white paint sealer. Chicago Leedys are unfinished mahogany with maple glue rings.

SNARE DRUMS

Shelly Manne: (Wood)
5½x14
wood shell
8 new separate-tension lugs
Stick Saver hoops
Broadway strainer

4½x14—same as 5½x14 with *Krupa* strainer

Broadway
6½x14, 8x14—same as 5½x14 but with a double row of
   small *Beavertail* lugs

Jack Sperling
5x14
brass shell in lacquer brass or chrome plated
8 new separate-tension lugs
Stick Saver hoops
Krupa strainer
(later called the *Joe Harris* model)

Ray Mosca
5½x14
wood shell
8 separate-tension lugs
Stick Saver hoops
Instant (*Rapid*) strainer
pearl or lacquer

Shelly Manne: (Metal)
5x14, 6½x14
chrome over brass shell
8 or 10 separate lugs
Stick Saver hoops
Broadway strainer

Irv Cottler
5x14, 6½x14
wood shell
8 or 10 separate-tension lugs
Stick Saver hoops
Instant strainer
pearl or lacquer

Aluminum Shell
5x14
6 separate-tension lugs
Stick Saver hoops
Instant strainer

Frank Capp
5½x14
same as *Ray Mosca* except available with 6 lugs
pearl or lacquer

Reliance
5½x14, 6½x14
mahogany shell
8 separate-tension lugs
single-flanged hoops with clips
Krupa strainer
mahogany, lacquer, or pearl

Utility
5½x14, 6½x14
mahogany shell
6 separate-tension lugs
flat hoops with clips
Krupa strainer
mahogany, lacquer, or pearl

Concert King
6½x14, 6½x15, 8x15
mahogany shell
16 *Beavertail* lugs
Stick Saver hoops
Broadway strainer
mahogany, lacquer, or pearl

Concert Snare
5½x14, 6½x14
mahogany shell
6 separate-tension lugs
6½x15 and 8x15 have 8 separate tension lugs
Instant strainer
Stick Saver hoops
mahogany, lacquer, or pearl

Tom-Toms And Bass Drums
Broadway
8x12, 9x13, 14x14, 16x16, 16x18, 18x20,
14x18, 14x20, 12x22, 14x22, 14x24, 14x26,
14x28, 16x30, 16x32, 16x34, 16x36
separate-tension *Beavertail* lugs
mahogany, lacquer or pearl

Note: Separate-tension tom-toms and bass
drums using center-mounted lugs were not
prominently illustrated in the catalogs, but
they did exist and used snare drum lugs.
There were drumset pictures to show the
mounted toms and bass drums. But no floor
toms were illustrated and no references to
any of the drums were listed in the respective tom-tom and bass drum pages.

Finishes
pearls and sparkles: white marine, light
blue, black diamond, silver sparkle, red
sparkle, aqua sparkle, blue sparkle, gold
sparkle, green sparkle, black sparkle, pink
sparkle, peacock sparkle, capri, fiesta, mardi
gras, black beauty (solid), blue agate, gray
agate, oyster pink, blue ripple, red ripple,
champagne
satin flames: white, red, blue, gold, green
lacquer: creme and green, blue and silver

Despite models named for major drummers (like this Shelly Manne kit shown in the 1965 catalog), Chicago-made Leedy drums were not successful.

Leedy & Ludwig

The World's Finest Drummers' Instruments

For about twenty years the management of C.G. Conn, Ltd. produced both Leedy and Ludwig & Ludwig drums. The two lines were run separately, but one can see that there are corresponding models for each price point and that the shells are identical. The only differences were in the hardware.

Some time after World War II, management at Conn began to wonder what they were doing with two drum companies. Sure, they could share workers and use the same stands and holders—but Conn was paying for two sales staffs and two sets of lug and strainer designs in chrome and in nickel. So in 1950, Conn announced the merger of these two giants, and the drum world was introduced to the drums of Leedy & Ludwig.

Unfortunately, this introduction forced many drum dealers out of business. It was a time of one dealer per town or specific geographic area. If a city had both a Leedy dealer and a Ludwig & Ludwig dealer, then somebody had to go, because there could only be one Leedy & Ludwig dealer.

All of the high-end drums carried Leedy hardware. The *Broadway* was retained as the top model, but Ludwig hardware was placed on the lower-cost products. The latter drums also used either single-flanged or flat hoops and clips.

In May of 1950, Leedy & Ludwig introduced a line of drums described as "revolutionary." These were the *Knob Tension* drums. Visually different, they were advertised as "mechanically perfect" and "scientifically engineered." Instead of rods for tensioning, these drums used knobs on the shell to tighten and loosen aluminum links that raised or lowered

The merger of Leedy and Ludwig was proudly announced in this 1950 flyer.

two inside rings. The rings pressed against the heads and increased the tension.

This description shows the ad man's delight: "As easy as dialing your own radio. No more 'clanking' drum keys to fumble with. Quick, positive finger-tip control. The knob with the slight bump (that you can feel in the dark) regulates the batter head. The plain knob is for the snare head. Turn right to tighten...left to loosen. To remove the heads, turn all large knobs to left to take off tension. Next remove all small knobs on the metal counter hoops. Lift off hoops. Heads are tucked in the conventional manner on either wood or metal flesh hoops. They are held in place by the flange on the inside of the metal counter hoop."

The April 1951 issue of *The Music Trades* stated that demand for the drums had exceeded company estimates. The story was accompanied by a picture of a set made for Sonny Greer, who had been a loyal Leedy user for almost thirty years. At the time of the picture, which is reproduced for this article, Greer was touring with a new band of former Duke Ellington sidemen.

In reality, the *Knob Tension* drums were a nightmare. Tom Jenkins, former sales manager of both Leedy and Leedy & Ludwig, told me that they were "the disaster of the century." The mechanism failed and there were many dissatisfied dealers and customers. Legend tells us that George Way was fired because of the *Knob Tension* fiasco, but that's not true—although he had been the promoter of the plan.

On one hand, it's interesting that George pushed the *Knob Tension* idea, because it had been tried twice before by Cecil Strupe (a former colleague of Way's)—and had failed each time. (See the chapters on L&S and WFL.) The only thing I can figure is that there was some good old-fashioned rivalry between Way and Strupe. I know that George Way was a designer and dreamer, and I have heard that he gave Cecil Strupe ideas for which he got no credit. Could George Way have thought the earlier "bugs" were fixed and that he could beat Strupe in the design department—or had the original master tension idea *come* from George Way and this was his opportunity to set things straight?

Before the official end in 1954, George Way left Leedy & Ludwig to become a manufacturer's rep. The company still had conventional drums to sell, but the court of execution was convening. By 1954, top management at Conn decided to con-

centrate on the manufacture of electric organs. Funding for that project would come from the sale of the drum division. The existing inventory was sold to Indiana Music, an Indianapolis retailer. The plant was leased to George Way, who planned the George Way Company. The Leedy dies and patents went to Slingerland for $90,000. The Ludwig & Ludwig dies and patents went to WFL for the same amount. The two hundred and fifty employees disappeared into the mist.

George Way was able to continue drum production in the Buescher Building for about six more years before the plant finally lost its connection to the drum world. The history of his company is detailed in chapter 14.

....

SNARE DRUMS

Broadway
5½x14, 6½x14, 8x14
16 *Beavertail* lugs
double-flanged hoops
chrome or nickel plating
Extension strainer
mahogany, lacquer, or pearl

Broadway New Era
4½x14
16 side-by-side *Beavertail* lugs
double-flanged hoops
chrome or nickel plating
Pioneer strainer
pearl, lacquer

Concert King
8x15
same information as *Broadway*

Reliance
5x14, 6½x14
8 Ludwig *Imperial* lugs
single-flange hoops with clips
nickel plating
Pioneer strainer
mahogany, pearl, lacquer, metal

Utility
5x14, 6½x14
6 Ludwig *Imperial* lugs
straight hoops with clips
nickel plating
Pioneer strainer
mahogany, lacquer

Nifty
3½x13
6 thumb rods
straight hoops with clips
nickel plating
Ludwig *Universal* snare strainer
mahogany, metal

TOM-TOMS

Broadway
8x12, 9x13, 16x16, 16x18, 18x20, 20x20
single-flanged hoops with clips
chrome or nickel plating
pearl, lacquer

BASS DRUMS

Broadway
14x20, 14x22, 14x24, 14x26, 14x28, 16x30, 16x32, 16x34, 16x36
large *Beavertail* lugs
inlaid hoops
chrome or nickel plating
pearl, lacquer, mahogany

Spartan
14x24, 14x26, 14x28, 16x30, 16x32, 16x34 (separate-tension)
14x24, 14x26, 14x28, 16x30 (single-tension)
large Ludwig *Imperial* lugs
maple or inlaid hoops
nickel plating
mahogany, pearl, lacquer

Knob Tension Drums
snare: 4½x14, 5½x14
toms: 9x13, 16x16
bass: 14x22, 14x24
chrome plating
available only in white marine and black diamond pearl

FINISHES
white marine, black diamond, gold sparkle, silver sparkle, green sparkle, red sparkle, blue sparkle, tri-tone blue, and silver lacquer

Leedy & Ludwig's unique—and unsuccessful—knob-tension tuning design was featured on this custom kit made for Sonny Greer in 1951.

Chapter 8

L&S (a.k.a. Leedy & Strupe)

Creators of Superior Percussion Instruments

When U.G. Leedy decided to sell the Leedy Manufacturing Company to C.G. Conn, Ltd., Leedy Manufacturing had over one hundred thousand square feet of space in the Indianapolis factory. Although U.G. had been assured that Conn would keep the plant open, by the next year operations had been moved to Elkhart, Conn's home base. Not all of the Leedy employees wanted to move north to Elkhart. Many of them remained in Indianapolis, so U.G. Leedy decided to help them. He formed a second company to make drums and other non-related products. The original name was to be "Leedy & Sons," but Conn's attorneys were less than enthusiastic, so the official name became "General Products Corporation, Manufacturers of L&S Drummers Equipment." Instead of "Leedy & Sons," the letters unofficially came to stand for "Leedy and Strupe." The Leedy was U.G.'s son Edwin "Hollis" Leedy and the Strupe was Cecil Strupe, the former chief engineer of Leedy Manufacturing.

Before the operation was under way, U.G. Leedy succumbed to heart disease. He was only sixty-three, but left a legacy of so many remarkable products that he filled two lifetimes. His wife and son wanted L&S to continue the Leedy tradition.

The first problem was the down time. The initial delivery of percussion products didn't start until October 1, 1931, over a year and a half after U.G. Leedy formed the company. Secondly, the two principals—Edward Hollis Leedy and Cecil Strupe—quite honestly detested each other. (I never met Strupe, but his photographs show a pretty serious-looking man. I have met Ed Leedy, and he is a jovial and charming man. But he still has no love for Strupe. I'm not giving away any secrets; Bill Ludwig, Jr. told me about the feud years before I ever saw an L&S drum or met Ed Leedy.)

U.G. Leedy had envisioned General Products as a guarantor of security for his former employees. (Remember, this was all unfolding during the Great Depression.) He saw the organization as more than a manufacturer of percussion items. He felt that it should build products on a contract basis for other firms as well as for itself. U.G. financed the whole thing. He bought a former dairy building on Orchard Avenue in Indianapolis and equipped it with a tool and die shop, a metalworking facility, and electro-plating and painting departments.

When Mr. Leedy died, the fate of General Products rested in the hands of Strupe and the other faithful. Mrs. Leedy stepped forward and finished the financing by donating enough money to set up a woodworking shop. L&S designed and built a full line of percussion and mallet products. They couldn't afford a sales staff, so a contract was signed with Chicago Musical Instrument Company for nationwide representation. Should you find an L&S catalog, you will notice the prominent listing of Chicago Musical Instrument Company as the national distributor.

The first major creation advertised by the company was modestly called "the greatest drum improvement in history." The *Strupe Master Tension* drum had two timpani rods jut-

The "L&S" on this badge originally stood for "Leedy & Sons," but legalities and other factors caused it to become known—at least unofficially— as standing for "Leedy & Strupe."

ting out of each shell. While rods were used to keep hoops on the drums, it was the handles that did the tensioning. One handle tightened each head. Here's the description:

"Operating on the principle of pedal timpani, these two handles provide full regulation for both heads. After the head is properly seated at the factory, no further adjustment of the individual rods with the key is necessary, excepting for seasonal regulations to take up stretch of heads."

The *Master Tension* series featured snare and bass drums as well as field drums. The snare drums were available with both wood and metal shells and had extension snares. Despite these features the *Master Tension* series was a complete failure.

L&S rods were slot-headed like those made by Leedy (Indianapolis), but the heads were hexagonal instead of round, so a special drumkey was used. (Some of the drums used a non-slot head, but the hexagonal shape seems to have been a constant.) L&S built a number of conventional drum models as well as their own pedals, stands, and other hardware. Herman Winterhoff (former Leedy vice president who is credited with creation of the vibraphone) also designed and built marimbas, bells, xylophones, and the "vibrato-phone," the L&S name for his vibraphone.

General Products struggled for nine years, but by 1939 the little company was about finished. Strupe—who had ignored the Leedy family and created ill will and tension—left in 1937. Ed Leedy left L&S to work for the Curtiss Wright Company, then later resigned to join the Navy. After the war he was hired by a Cincinnati firm that manufactured commercial baking equipment. He stayed there until his retirement.

Cecil Strupe moved from Indianapolis and joined WFL in Chicago, where he became that company's chief engineer. There he invented the triple-flanged hoop as well as the *Victorious* line of drums. (Both of these are detailed in the chapter on WFL.) Since the War Production Board had controls on critically needed raw materials, drum manufacturers went into nearly total hibernation. So Strupe went to Cleveland, Ohio and joined the White Musical Instrument Company, whose factory was converted to war item production. After the war, Strupe remained at White, but he had disappeared from the world of percussion.

SNARE DRUMS

Master Tension
5x14, 6½x14, 6½x15
8 *Master Tension* (rigid) lugs
double-flanged hoops
chrome or nickel plating
dual-plane strainer (extension)

L&S built these other models as well:
Dictator, Rhythm King, Service, Transient, Concert, Reliable, and the *Boys School*
sizes ranged from 3½x12 to 6½x15

As late as 1936, L&S did not make tunable tom-toms.

FINISHES

black lacquer, white lacquer, a combination of the two called ivory and jet (black drums with white diamonds), white marine pearl, black diamond pearl, silver, gold, and green sparkle

L&S could not maintain a sales staff, so the products were represented by Chicago Musical Instrument Company.

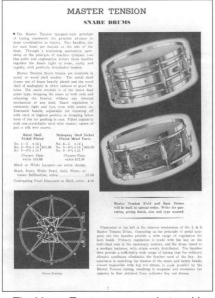

The Master Tension system—designed by Cecil Strupe in the early 1930s—utilized timpani-like rods and handles for tuning purposes. It was a complete failure.

This 1937 Dictator snare drum represented the pinnacle of L&S's achievement. By 1939 the company was virtually finished.

Chapter 9

Ludwig Drum Company

The Most Famous Name On Drums

The year was 1955. The competitors were Gretsch, Rogers, Slingerland, and WFL. Leedy & Ludwig had ceased manufacturing and was for sale. Bill Ludwig, Jr. must have been thrilled at the chance to reunite the Ludwig name with the Ludwig family. Bill Senior was on a trip to Florida when Bill Junior contacted him. Junior wanted to spend the money. Senior had mixed feelings. It was a lot to spend—but there was power in the name. The finished drums had been sold to an Indianapolis music store, but the tooling, dies, and patents were for sale for $180,000. The Ludwigs went for it and spent half the requested amount to buy the Ludwig & Ludwig side of the house. H.H. "Bud" Slingerland, Jr. bought the Leedy half. (See chapter 6: Leedy—Chicago.)

The 1956 catalog shows both brand names on the cover: Ludwig in an oval and WFL in a keystone. WFL badges continued to be used until about 1959. By then the badge was changed to a larger keystone with the Ludwig name in a blue oval. This is called the "Transition Badge" and was used until the supply was exhausted in about a year. The stockpile of products stamped with the WFL logo lasted into the mid '60s.

In the 1956 to 1960 time frame, Ludwig/WFL was in a good position. The Ludwig name was back, Buddy Rich was the top endorser, a young Joe Morello was on the way up, and there were lots of other stars. The dealer group expanded, because the company was able to reconnect with old-line Ludwig & Ludwig dealers. (The most collectible snare drum from this period is the *Supraphonic* made in brass. Later drums were fabricated from alloys, and although they're still collectible, they're worth only a third of the brass snare. Collector interest in the brass *Supraphonic* played a part in the reintroduction of brass shells for high-end Ludwig snare drums in 1994.)

The senior and junior Ludwigs added on to the Damen Avenue factory in Chicago eight times between 1956 and 1966 and increased the company's output. The look, the name, and the quality of the drums made Ludwig popular with over three thousand dealers around the world.

In 1963 Ludwig's English distributor, Ivor Arbiter, displayed an oyster black set. It was seen by a young Liverpudlian who decided that he had to have those drums—if something could be customized. Richard "Ringo Starr" Starkey wanted to show that his new

drums were imported, so he asked that a larger Ludwig logo be painted on his front bass head. When Ringo bought those Ludwigs, he couldn't have dreamed that he would be the reason that literally millions of young people would take up the drums as a result of his appearance with the Beatles on *The Ed Sullivan Show* in February, 1964. Those kids bought a lot of drums, and a big percentage of those drums were Ludwigs. Bill Ludwig, Jr. presented Ringo with a 14-karat gold plated *Super Sensitive* in 1964 as a token of appreciation to his best unpaid salesman.

In the 1960s Ludwig could do no wrong. Most of the major acts used Ludwig drums. Even drummers who endorsed other brands often used Ludwig snare drums. During the Beatles craze, the factory was running three shifts a day, six days a week, building one hundred four-piece sets each work day.

The Ludwigs resurrected the *Ludwig Drummer* and continued it through the 1970s. The issues weren't mailed; they were sent to music stores, where the faithful would go to get them. The same was

The founder and the heir apparent of a drum dynasty:
the two William F. Ludwigs in 1959

true for the catalogs.

Ludwig catalogs were always to be cherished. Bill Jr. has written about the many times parents would tell him of the child who fell asleep re-reading a Ludwig catalog. Kids in the 1960s literally memorized each page. I could quote part numbers, set names, and illustrated colors. Each new catalog was devoured, and we looked for any changes from the last edition. One set that was always there was the *Blue Note,* billed as the ultimate in modern outfits. Initially covered in sky blue pearl, and then blue sparkle, the *Blue Note* had double bass, two ride toms, two floor toms, a wood shell snare, bongos, and a matching seat case. In 1967 it listed for $1,000. Where do I send my check?

Bill Junior laughed at me in April, 1994, when I told him I had spent $95 to buy a 1960 catalog. He couldn't believe it. I told him they had thrown away a fortune when they tossed out the old catalogs.

In the early '60s the "Keystone" badges did not have serial numbers. By 1963, the U. S. Government required them. Many collectors seek out the "pre-serial number" Ludwigs trying to find the brass *Supraphonics.* Most of the wood shells from 1956 to the early 1960s are made with three plies of unfinished mahogany and poplar and are fitted with maple reinforcing hoops. Toward the end of the '60s an off-white sealer began to be used on the insides of the shells, followed later by a clear coat. Finally the shells featured a clear coat and no reinforcing rings. For many of those years, an inked date stamp was applied.

Ludwig was the last major company to start using only chrome for plating. So you may find a set with one tom plated in nickel and one in chrome. Odds are the chrome one was added later.

By the end of the '60s the company needed a model with which to fight import brands, so they introduced the *Standard* line. The name dated back to a snare model introduced by Ludwig & Ludwig in the 1920s. The only other line of drums made by Ludwig was the *Club Date,* whose shells were the same as the *Super Classic. Club Dates* had center-mounted separate-tension lugs on the bass drums and toms. The *Standards* had their own distinctive hardware, pedal, hi-hat, stands, holder, and mounts. The interiors of the shells were finished in *Granitone*—a gray speckled material. The colors were different from those in the pro lines and, of course, the prices were much lower. The *Standards* were not successful, but the lugs were later reintroduced for the *Rocker* line.

The challenges to the Ludwig Drum Company have been many, but it's still the longest-lived drum company in the United States. In 1968 the old trademark was retired and a streamlined design of the name was adopted. The Ludwig Drum Company became known as Ludwig Industries, since they also owned Musser, Kitching, and the William Schuessler Case Co. It was quite a company.

The most collectible Ludwig drums are: the brass-shelled *Supraphonic* in chrome or clear lacquer, the *Super Classic* 5½x14 with *Classic* strainer, and the *Downbeat* 4x14.

SNARE DRUMS 1950s

Buddy Rich Super Classic
5½x14
8 *Classic* lugs
triple-flanged hoops
nickel, chrome plating
Classic strainer
pearl, lacquer

Festival Model
6½x14, 6½x15, 8x15
16 small *Classic* lugs
triple-flanged hoops
nickel, chrome plating
P83 strainer
pearl, lacquer, mahogany

Barrett Deems
same as *Buddy Rich* except *P83* strainer

Symphonic
5½x14, 6½x14
16 small *Classic* lugs
triple-flanged hoops
nickel, chrome plating
Classic strainer
pearl, lacquer

Concert Model
6½x14, 6½x15, 8x15
8 *Classic* lugs
triple-flanged hoops
nickel, chrome plating
P83 strainer
pearl, lacquer, mahogany

Supreme Concert
5½x14, 6½x14
6 *Classic* lugs
triple-flanged hoops
nickel plating
P83 strainer
lacquer, mahogany

Be Bop
3x13
6 *Piccolo* lugs
triple-flanged hoops
chrome plating only
Be Bop strainer
pearl only

The first Ludwig catalog that appeared after William F. Ludwig Jr. bought the family name back in 1955 featured the Ludwig script logo in an oval, but also retained the WFL "Keystone" logo.

Compacto
4x14
8 *Piccolo* lugs
triple-flanged hoops
chrome plating only
Be Bop strainer
pearl only

Super Porto Pak
5½x13
6 *Classic* lugs
triple-flanged hoops
nickel, chrome plating
P83 strainer
pearl only

Classic Porto Pak
same as *Super Porto Pak* except
 Classic strainer

Super All Metal
6½x14
non-beaded shell
6 Classic lugs
triple-flanged hoops
nickel plating
P83 strainer

BASS DRUMS

Super Classic
14x20, 12x22, 14x22, 14x24, 14x26, 14x28, 14x30, 16x32
Classic lugs
separate-tension
nickel, chrome plating
pearl, lacquer, mahogany

Standard
14x28 only
single-tension
center stud/long T-rods
lacquer, mahogany

Concert
14x22, 14x24, 14x28 only

separate tension:
center-mounted *Classic* lugs
nickel, chrome plating
pearl, mahogany, lacquer

single-tension:
center-mounted *Classic* lugs with long T-rods
nickel plating
lacquer, mahogany

TOM-TOMS

Super Classic
8x12, 9x13, 12x14, 14x14, 16x16, 16x18, 18x20
separate-tension *Classic* lugs
triple-flanged hoops
nickel, chrome plating
pearl, lacquer

Club Date
8x12, 9x13, 12x15, 14x14
separate-tension center-mount *Classic* lugs
triple-flanged hoops
nickel, chrome plating
lacquer only initially, then pearl

FINISHES

white marine pearl, black diamond pearl, sparkling gold, sparkling green, sparkling red, sparkling blue, sparkling silver, jet black ebony pearl, blue & silver lacquer, black & gold lacquer, sky blue, oyster pink, oyster black, oyster blue, pink champagne, sparkling burgundy, galaxy, psychedelic red, mod orange, citrus mod, black panther

SNARE DRUMS 1960s

Supraphonic
5x14, 6½x14
chrome or clear lacquer over brass shell (later chrome over alloy shell)
10 *Imperial* lugs
triple-flanged hoops
P83 strainer

Super Sensitive
same as *Supraphonic* but with *P70* parallel strainer

Jazz Festival
5x14
8 *Classic* lugs
triple-flanged hoops
nickel, chrome plating
P83 strainer
pearl, lacquer

The so-called "Transition Badge" incorporated the script Ludwig name on the "Keystone" badge shape. These badges only lasted about a year, from 1959 through 1960.

Ringo Starr was Ludwig's best unpaid salesman. He is credited with inspiring literally millions of young people to play—and buy—drums (a large proportion of which were Ludwigs).

Touted as "the ulimate in modern outfits," the Ludwig Blue Note kit was considered huge in 1967.

Acrolite
5x14
alloy shell with aluminum finish
8 *Classic* lugs
triple-flanged hoops
chrome plating
P83 strainer

Pioneer
5x14, 6½x14
6 *Classic* lugs
triple-flanged hoops
nickel, chrome plating
large *Pioneer* (*P85*) strainer (later *P83*)
mahogany, lacquer

Auditorium
(replaces *Contest* model)
6½x14, 6½x15, 8x15
P85 strainer
pearl, mahogany, lacquer

LUDWIG STANDARDS

Snare
5x14
8 *Standard* lugs
triple-flanged hoops
P83 strainer
(metal) chrome or *Acrolite* finish
(wood) pearl finish

Bass
14x20, 14x22
(14x22 single-head also available)

Tom-Toms
double-head: 8x12, 9x13, 14x14, 16x16
single-head: 5$\frac{1}{2}$x8, 5x12, 5x13, 11x16

FINISHES

gold strata, blue strata, bronze strata, ruby strata, lemon strata, avocado strata, silver mist, gold mist, red mist, blue mist, silver astro, blue astro, red astro, charcoal astro, gold astro

The Standard series was introduced in the late '60s to combat import brands. It was not successful, but the lugs were used later in the Rocker series.

Chapter 10

Ludwig & Ludwig

Drum Makers to the Profession • Drum Standard of the World • Tops in the Drum World

In 1909, William F. Ludwig, Sr. and his younger brother Theobald were living in the bustling city of Chicago. Rebuilt after the "Great Fire" of 1871, Chicago was teeming with people lured by the promise of opportunity. The Ludwigs were working drummers who also represented Leedy Manufacturing in Chicago—selling Leedy snare drums and traps from a sixth floor office in the Omaha Building. While in his twenties, Bill had two experiences that ultimately affected drummers for generations to come.

The first episode happened in 1902, in Buffalo, New York. Young Bill was performing a snare drum duet with a famous drummer named Tom Mills. Mills was playing a European-made, separate-tension $6^1/_2$x13 brass-shelled snare drum. It was tensioned with bolts that passed through studs welded on each hoop and into a second set screwed into the shell. Inside the shell (and connected to the studs) were metal plates used to reinforce the drum against the tremendous pressure caused by tuning. Although it was quite crude by today's standards, when Mills played this snare drum in the duet with Ludwig, the sound of his clear, crisp playing covered over the best attempts the twenty-three-year-old Ludwig could get from his wood shell. Bill made up his mind that he would own the Tom Mills snare drum. Two years later—so the story goes—Bill met Mills again. Mills was down on his luck and when Ludwig reminded him that he'd still like the brass snare, Mills took a pawn ticket from his pocket and handed it to Ludwig. The drum was redeemed for $3. When Bill played the drum it reinforced his desire to see such instruments in the hands of more players.

The second fateful event occurred during a performance of *The Follies* of 1908, when Bill found himself unable to play four-to-the-bar on a bass drum during a ragtime number. In the bands of the 19th century—such as the Sousa

William F. Ludwig, Sr., shown in 1926

The "other" Ludwig was William's brother Theo, who died in the influenza epidemic of 1918 at the age of twenty-nine.

band—one drummer played snare, a second played bass drum, and a third played traps. The drumset did not exist until the 20th century, and the first attempts at making practical bass drum pedals were awful. Bill Ludwig was a victim of this situation. He was using a Leedy *Swing* pedal that was considered the best available. But it had thirty-five parts including a rod that ran the length of the back bass-drum head and was connected to a footboard at the bottom. The beater was suspended from the top of this contraption. Deciding to solve his own problem, Bill carved a wooden pedal. That pedal was later mass-produced in metal, and the Ludwig & Ludwig firm was in business. They billed themselves as "Ludwig & Ludwig, Chicago's Only Exclusive Drum Shop."

The first catalog was published in 1911. It listed the Ludwig patent pedal, the Ludwig metal drum (based on the Mills drum), the Ludwig patent snare strainer (misspelled, by the way, as "stainer"), Ludwig drumheads, Ludwig sound effects, and Ludwig fiber cases. Besides brief professional biographies of the brothers, there was a listing of K Zildjian cymbals and the following sentence: "Our stock includes a full line of the celebrated Leedy drums, bells, timpanies, xylophones, and traps. Ask for a Leedy catalog if you have none."

As you might guess, the affiliation with Leedy ended when Bill and Theo became first-rate manufacturers. Their sister came on board to do the books, and her husband, Robert C. Danly, volunteered to be their engineer.

Danly's contribution to the firm's success was critical. He designed the one product that set Ludwig & Ludwig apart from the competition: the strainer. Lots of companies had great shells, there are European snare drums with tube lugs that predate the 1912 Ludwigs (their 1909-1911 models used studs without the tube to connect them), and Duplex probably had separate tension first. But no one had as quiet and strong a strainer, because no one else had Danly. It's no wonder that Ludwig grew rapidly. Each of the strainer models was better than those produced by any other company, with their dependability being the overriding factor.

Both Bill and Theo had continued playing, but Theo became more of a "homebody" to mind the business. During World War I, Ludwig & Ludwig was awarded a marching-drum order by the U.S. Army. The order was then canceled and given to Gretsch. (Someone had changed the specifications in shell size after the Ludwigs had won the bidding.) Theo took off for Washington by train. Unfortunately, he did not win back the order—and he contracted the flu. It was 1918, during the Great Influenza Epidemic, when twenty-five million people died. One of them was Theobald Ludwig, age twenty-nine.

Ludwig & Ludwig faced its first crisis. Bill left his job at the Chicago Symphony and Danly left his at International Harvester. There was no looking back.

From the end of World War I to 1930 the firm's success came from the growth of live music, pit orchestras, and the rising importance of drum corps. Ludwig & Ludwig made drums and banjos and launched two newsletters: *The Ludwig Drummer* and the *Ludwig Banjoist*. The latter was short-lived, but the *Drummer* had forty-one issues. (Bill Sr. later took an active role in and was a charter member of the National Association of Rudimental Drummers [NARD], founded in 1933. Use of the rudiments was one of the keystones of the drum corps movement.)

Pit musicians, Shriners, Legionnaires, and high schools bought a lot of drums throughout the 1920s. But two major events at the end of the decade forced Ludwig & Ludwig to face its second major crisis. The first event came in 1927, when Warner Brothers released Al Jolson's *The Jazz Singer*. When Jolson sang from the screen, sound came to film, and lots of musicians became unemployed. And then, in 1929, the stock market collapsed.

Danly left Ludwig & Ludwig to run a die-making business that he had quietly started with his sons in the basement of the drum factory. Bill approached C.D. Greenleaf, the president of C.G. Conn, Ltd., and sold Ludwig & Ludwig for $1,000,000 worth of Conn Stock. (U.G. Leedy had gotten to Greenleaf first and had taken all his cash for the purchase of Leedy.)

One of Bill Ludwig's requests was that the factory remain in Chicago. Greenleaf agreed—and then had it moved to the Buescher Building in Elkhart, Indiana, the same location used by Leedy. Leedy and Ludwig & Ludwig used the same machinery and shells for the next twenty years, until they were formally merged as Leedy & Ludwig in 1950.

Conn kept a Ludwig & Ludwig sales force in Chicago and continued to use an oval Chicago badge until after World War II—at which time the Elkhart badge was unveiled. It may not be fair to say that Conn didn't reveal the truth. They simply chose to say very little. To the consumer it looked like William F. Ludwig, Sr. was still in charge in Chicago.

But he was not in charge. He became a minority stockholder, taking orders. Leedy sales manager Tom Jenkins told me that Conn viewed Leedy as "top dog," and drum legend says that Bill had to

This brass-shelled snare drum, christened the "Tom Mills" after its original owner, inspired William F. Ludwig, Sr. to create metal-shelled snare drums.

fight with Conn over appropriations and new products. Years after the fact he wrote: "Since everyone found it hard to reconcile my feelings regarding drum construction and management of the new setup with those of the new owners, I therefore, in 1936, left the employ of the Conn Company on amicable terms."[1]

The Bill Ludwig, Sr. story continues in the WFL and Ludwig chapters. For now, we return to the story of the Ludwig & Ludwig company.

The Leedy division had unveiled the X lug in 1930 as the first truly self-aligning lug. Ludwig & Ludwig continued to use tube lugs. But with the advent of the Conn design, in 1935-36 Ludwig introduced the *Silver Anniversary* drums. Available in a seamless brass or solid mahogany shell, the *Anniversary* models brought Ludwig & Ludwig into parity with its sister company. The *Imperial* lug did not swivel, because the lug nuts were flush with the top of the lug. But it was progress and it became the most popular snare drum lug of all time. The *Imperial* lug (with different lug nuts and a rounded cut-out) is still used on *Supraphonics, Super Sensitives,* and full-size *Black Beauties.*

In the 1920s Ludwig & Ludwig had been the first company to have fancy finishes: gold-plated drums and drums covered in *Ludwigold*—a stucco-like gold sparkle that was baked on. The company also developed the first snare drum with two sets of snares.

In the '30s and '40s, the Conn-owned company was content to sell snare drums and kits in traditional sizes and finishes without much worry about being on the cutting edge. Like Leedy, Ludwig & Ludwig gave up solid shells for those with plies. Their biggest worry seemed to be the presence of Bill Ludwig, Sr. and his little upstart WFL Drum Company.

First, Conn threatened to sue Ludwig for using his own last name. Then, in 1940, they wrote: "**Beware of Imitations**. We regret that recently customers have complained of receiving unsatisfactory merchandise which, investigation revealed, was not made or manufactured by us, although the customer erroneously thought he had purchased genuine Ludwig & Ludwig equipment.... Note: Do not confuse the genuine Ludwig & Ludwig, Inc. percussion or mallet-played instruments and accessories, which we manufacture, with any other products bearing a similar name of company or individual."[2]

World War II put off the drum battles for over four years. Ludwig & Ludwig built wood-shell/wood-lug drums called the *Victory* Line. In 1946 and 1947 updated price lists still used the 1941 catalog for illustrations. A new catalog was released in 1948, although there were no new products. In 1950 Ludwig & Ludwig disappeared into the combined firm of Leedy & Ludwig, where it stayed until the 1955 buy-out by the Ludwig family that ultimately created the modern Ludwig Drum Company.

While a traditionalist may say that Ludwig & Ludwig ceased to exist the day Bill Sr. left, there are a number of great drums from the 1936 to 1950 time period. In the Leedy & Ludwig phase, Ludwig & Ludwig hardware was only placed on low-cost models. Let's go over the drums sold from 1920 through 1949.

1. *My Life At The Drums*—pamphlet by William F. Ludwig, published by the Ludwig Drum Company
2. Ludwig & Ludwig catalog—1940

SNARE DRUMS 1920-1929

All Metal Separate-Tension
5x14, 6½x14, 6½x15, 5x15, 4x14, 4x15
two-piece shell with center bead
initially 6 tube lugs, then 8, then 10
flat then single-flanged hoops with clips
initially nickel plating, then
    Deluxe (imitation gold),
    chrome (1929 on),
    gold, and *Ludwigold*
Professional (*Pioneer*) strainer

Wood Shell Separate-Tension
solid-wood shell
same sizes and information as metal
    shell
6 tube lugs

Thumb Rod Orchestra Drum
maple shell
16 rods
wooden counterhoops
Professional strainer mounted on the
    top initially, then center-mounted
mahogany, walnut

Ten Thumb Rods
Small Orchestra/Parlor Drums
same as above but with 10 rods
metal or wooden counterhoops
6 thumb rods
hoop-mounted *Professional* strainer
mahogany or walnut

Super Ludwig
5x14, 6½x14, 6½x15,
5x15, 4x14, 4x15
solid wood (walnut) in mahogany,
    maple, white or black enamel, or
    nickel over brass shell with
    center bead
10 tube lugs
parallel throwoff
pearl available in late '20s

Super Sensitive
5x14, 6½x14, 6½x15
metal with center bead or solid
    mahogany shell with 10 tube lugs
    until 1936
single-flanged hoops with clips
parallel strainer, second strainer
    under batter head
nickel, chrome plating
pearl

Pioneer
4x14, 5x14, 4x15, 5x15
metal with bead or maple or
    mahogany shell
8 lugs
flat hoops withclips
Pioneer strainer

The original Ludwig & Ludwig metal bass drum pedal was a vast improvement over other models of its day (circa 1908). It helped to establish the company as a manufacturer of quality percussion products.

Ludwig & Ludwig's Combination (above) and Pioneer model (below) strainers set them apart from other drum manufacturers.

Universal
5x14
center-beaded shell or wood shell (maple, mahogany)
6 tube lugs
hoop-mounted *Universal* strainer

New Era Sensitive
3x12, 3x13, 3x14, 3x15, 4x14, 4x15,
5x14, 5x15
metal or mahogany shell
two strainers: snares on bottom of
    top head and on top of bottom head

Junior Orchestra
3½x13
wood or metal shell with bead
6 thumb rods
hoop-mounted *Universal* strainer
nickel plating

Juvenile School
3x12, 3x13
wood or nickel-plated metal shell
6 thumb rods
Universal strainer

Note: The *Black Beauty* (Ludwig *Deluxe*) was available using the *All Metal* snare, the *Super Ludwig*, or the *Super Sensitive* (including the *New Era*). Each drum could also be finished in white enamel, *Ludwigold*, gold, or gold that was hand burnished. See finishes.

BASS DRUMS 1920-1929

Dance Model
(later *Dance* and *Tango*)
mahogany or maple shell with
    maple hoops
thumb rods, then later
    timpani-handled rods
single-tension

Center Support
(later called *Artist's Special*)
12x24 to 16x34
laminated mahogany, maple,
    or walnut shell
single-tension
also available in black or white enamel

Separate-Tension
(later called *Aerokraft Construction*)
laminated mahogany with maple hoops
double studs
thumb rods then timpani-handled rods

Double Stud
same as *Separate-Tension* except used
    thumb rods, then timpani-handled
    rods on one side and single
    claws on the other

Rope and combination rod-and-rope
    models also available.

Universal
maple shell or mahogany on special order
center support
thumb rods on one side, single claw on the other,
    then timpani-handled rods

Universal "Dance Type" or "Tango Type"
maple shell or mahogany on special order
thumb rods, then timpani-handled rods
no center support
single claws

Pioneer
mahogany shell or maple with maple counterhoops
double studs and timpani handles
naturally finished

Pioneer Center Supports
(also without center supports)
same as *Pioneer* with either one center stud or none at all

Super-Aerokraft
(later the *Super Bass*)
5 plies of mahogany
walnut and black enamel

Ludwig & Ludwig's 25th anniversary flyer touted the company's historical achievements and "teased" the market with the promise of a special new model to be introduced in 1935.

The mystery drum was christened the Silver Anniversary model. It featured the famous Ludwig Imperial lug.

TOM-TOMS 1920-1929
Chinese Tacked Heads
4x10, 6x12, 7x15, 9x13, 12x14, 16x16

FINISHES 1920-1929
Snare Drums
Deluxe: metal was shiny brass onto which a gold-tinted
    lacquer was sprayed
Ludwigold: a baked-on stucco-like gold finish
    (later called *Classic Gold*)
Triumph: 14-karat gold plating and then hand burnishing

Toms and Bass Drums
Pearls: avalon (white marine) pearl, streaked opal, peacock
pearl, rose pearl, golden flash, hotsy-totsy (red onyx)
mottled sepia
Enamel: black, white

SNARE DRUMS 1930-1939
In 1936, all Ludwig snares, except the *Pioneer* (8 lugs),
Universal (6 lugs), *Junior* (6 rods), and *Juvenile* (6 rods),
went from tube lugs to *Imperial* lugs. Solid shells were discontinued in favor of laminated shells.

NEW MODELS
Super Swing
6½x14 originally, 7x14, 8x14 by 1939
mahogany shell with maple hoops
8 lugs
pearl-inlaid wood counterhoops with double claws
    until 1939, then double-flanged hoops
nickel or chrome plating
Parallel strainer
natural mahogany or pearl

Standard Swing
same as *Super* except *Professional* strainer and 7x14 only,
    8x14 available by 1939 for one year using
    new *Standard* (non-extension) strainer

Concert
8x15
mahogany shell with mahogany finish
maple or double-flanged hoops
nickel plating

BASS DRUMS 1930-1939
By 1937, large *Imperial* lugs replaced tube lugs on separate-tension Ludwig *Standard* bass drums, the new name for separate-tension bass drums. A snare-drum-size *Imperial* lug acted as a center support for the Ludwig *Standard* single-tension model.

TOM-TOMS 1930-1939
Tom-Toms
7x11, 9x13, 12x14, 14x16
single- and separate-tension
single-flanged or wood counterhoops
tacked bottom heads onsingle-tension drums
center-mounted lugs on 11", 13", and 14" toms,
    16" has one row of lugs on top and one row on bottom

FINISHES 1930-1939
pearls: abalone, silver flash, black avalon (black diamond),
red flash, green flash, gold flash
enamel: hi-luster blue, hi-luster green, blue/silver,
black/gold

SNARE DRUMS 1940-1949

Ludwig Standard
adds 5½x14
adopts the "New Design Strainer" (non-extension) in early
  1940 and then adds extension bridges

Pioneer
adds 6½x14
metal or wood shell

Pioneer Concert
7x15
mahogany shell
8 tube lugs

Universal
Adds 6½x14
Pioneer strainer, then changes to new *Standard* strainer
nickel plating only

Universal Concert
6½x14
mahogany shell
6 tube lugs
flat hoops with clips
natural or white lacquer

BASS DRUMS 1940-1949

remains unchanged

TOM-TOMS 1940-1949

7x10, 9x13 single-headed models
pressed steel (airline) lugs
flat hoops with clips

add 16x16 standard model
8x12 standard model deleted
9x13 tube lug with tacked bottom heads added (*Artist* model)

FINISHES 1940-1949

by 1939, enamels were replaced with lacquers: green and
gold, red and silver, black and silver
Moderne series—blue and gray, tan and brown, black and
gold

Note: The *Moderne* series employed plastic lug casings using
what was called the *Bi-Tone* system. Drums were one color,
lugs the other. (Snare was a 6½x14 *Pioneer*, toms were
7x11, 9x13 with tacked bottom heads, bass was single-tension 14x26)

Note: From 1946 to 1950, the Ludwig & Ludwig badge used
Elkhart as the city of origin.

Chapter 11

The Rogers Drum Company

I have a real soft spot for Rogers. What started out as a third-rate drum company became a world-class competitor before it disappeared into the history books. And for one brief moment, the Rogers Drum Company out-engineered all of its rivals.

The names of three men are intertwined during the Rogers heyday. Henry Grossman bought the company in 1952, and moved it from New Jersey to Ohio. Joe Thompson designed products unlike anything the percussion world had seen. (He was so important to Henry Grossman that the new plant was built on Thompson's land in Covington, Ohio, for his convenience.) Joe brought us *Swiv-O-Matic* and *Dyna-Sonic* products, but Ben Strauss, as marketing manager, gave us the names and the ads and the sales momentum. He visited the drummers to find out what they needed. He even personally selected and weighed Buddy Rich's sticks. But let's go back to the beginning.

Joseph Rogers, Sr. left Ireland, no doubt during the potato famine, and came to the United States, knowing one trade. As a boy, he had worked at the Dublin Parchment Yards and had learned the old-world secret of making fine drumheads. He founded his own company in Farmingdale, New Jersey in 1849, and his heads were much in demand by the Union Army for their marching drums during the Civil War. His son, Joseph Jr., was his successor, and then, in 1929, control went to grandson Cleveland Rogers. The Rogers firm's specialty was always drum and banjo heads, and their products were found on other companies' drums. Conversely, other companies' drums were found in the Rogers catalog. A late '30s edition clearly illustrates Gretsch round-badge snare drums. Other drums have Slingerland and Duplex strainers. I have surmised that trade-outs occurred quite often.

In 1940, Cleveland Rogers wrote that many drummers quietly used Rogers. He was "content to let our success rest on the superior quality and performance of Rogers drums rather than on how loudly we can proclaim the names of those who use them."

In reality, Rogers was not a major drum manufacturer. They were a head manufacturer that assembled some drums and sold ready-made models built elsewhere. By the early 1950s, Cleveland Rogers was ill and his factory was a shambles. That's when Henry Grossman came in to buy the company from him. So the eagle-badged drums would now be made in Ohio and sold through Grossman's distribution system.

Grossman Music had become a giant by selling products to music stores. Those products could be private-labeled or could carry the distributor's name. At one time Ludwig & Ludwig drums were sold through such "jobbers," as were the drums of the Leedy Indianapolis spin-off, L&S.

Ben Strauss had joined the Grossman empire in 1937 and had managed the retail side of the business. His involvement with Rogers came about because he critiqued the early products from the Covington factory. He didn't think they were up to par with the Ludwig & Ludwig drums he had sold retail. Henry Grossman and Joe Thompson listened—and from that moment Ben became officially indispensable.

The executives at Grossman were out to build a great company. But they had inherited the designs of the Rogers Company—including the two worst-performing lug designs in history. These were the infamous drawn-brass lugs. First, there was a flat and then a ridged model. The latter design is often called the bread-and-butter lug. I have looked at hundreds of them, and almost every one is cracked. Ben Strauss said they worked fine—"until you tightened them." Hairline cracks became chasms...the bottoms would fall out...the tops would cave in. They were good-looking, but they were bad lugs.

This is where Joe Thompson enters the Rogers story. While operating a music store in the late 1930s Joe invented the Thompson Mouthpiece Puller for brass instruments. One of Grossman's salesman saw

Marketing manager Ben Strauss coined many of the most famous Rogers model names, including Swiv-O-Matic and Dyna-Sonic.

Joe Thompson was the design genius responsible for most of Rogers' major innovations.

it and took the idea back to Henry. That began the relationship. (Actually, Rogers employed the talents of lots of Buckeye craftsman over the years. The lugs were made in Cincinnati, the hoops were spun in Dayton, and other hardware was fashioned in Piqua.)

Joe Thompson redesigned the Rogers spurs, cymbal holders, tom-tom legs and mounts—and finally the lug. (Hurray!) The *Beavertail* lug that was introduced about 1963 was a long time in coming, but it's a great-looking piece of engineering and it doesn't crack.

Joe also introduced a practical ball-and-socket arrangement for tom-tom and cymbal mounts that is so logical it's hard to believe that no one thought of it before. This was the legendary *Swiv-O-Matic* system.

With the *Swiv-O-Matic* system, everything is tightened with a drumkey. (Ben told me that after sales meetings, the beer was bought by the guy who forgot to bring his key. It was the most important sales aid a Rogers salesman could carry.) The idea for the system came from camera tripods. However, Thompson improved on it by making the ball egg-shaped, with set screws above center to force the ball down into the pocket.

Henry Grossman believed that "it takes a good name to sell a product." Henry apparently liked to carry a folder into which he placed names for products when he needed one. During a train ride from Sidney, Ohio to Cleveland (Covington didn't have a train stop), Grossman and Strauss first came up with *Swivel-Matic*, then changed it to *Swiv-O-Matic*.

Joe Thompson built on two ideas from early Leedy catalogs. The first one suggested that a drummer could avoid stands by hooking everything together. Using the *Swiv-O-Matic* hex rods, the snare drum was connected to the bass drum in such a way that the drummer could pick up the bass, tom, cymbal, and snare in one hand and carry the floor tom in the other. Cleveland area drummer Howard Brush posed with the system in a number of catalogs, as did national star Cozy Cole. That idea didn't catch on—but a second idea did. That idea was to have a snare drum whose snares were always under tension. Instead of lowering the snares, the drummer would lower the unit that *held* the snares. Leedy had introduced the *Marvel* snare drum with such a system in 1925, but the world wasn't ready for it. The Rogers version was called the *Dyna-Sonic*, and it was immediately accepted. Available in metal or wood, the *Dyna-Sonic* was first an eight- and then a ten-lug top-of-the-line model. It retailed for $150—at a time when Slingerland and Ludwig each charged $100 or less for their top snare drums.

Ben Strauss told me that the *Dyna-Sonic* was originally designed for Buddy Rich. Buddy wanted a drum that could go from pianissimo to forte, be extremely resonant, and never choke. The *Dyna-Sonic* answered Buddy's demand, with its precision snare bed, *Diplomat* batter head, and frame-mounted snares always parallel to the snare head. Again, Ben exercised his penchant for descriptive names: "Dynamic Sound"=*Dyna-Sonic*.

The drum was the talk of the industry. One day, Ben Strauss received a call from one of his dealers. Could Rogers build a *Dyna-Sonic* and cover it in white pearl—but not put any hardware on it? Curious but patient, Ben had it built and

sent. The dealer drilled the shell, installed Slingerland hardware on it, and sent the drum to Gene Krupa with all the secrecy of a government spy plot. But that telltale frame below the snare head was a dead giveaway, and some drum spy finked on Gene. Bud Slingerland made the call and Krupa went back to his *Radio King*.

Buddy joined Rogers in 1960, after thirteen years as a Ludwig endorser. Rogers shipped a set to dealer Ellis Tollin at Music City in Philadelphia for Buddy to use with his quintet. Buddy's creeping Walberg hi-hat was modified on the spot by Strauss and Tobin—and the first hi-hat spur was created. Buddy was with Rogers for six years. He left them in 1966 when CBS Records let him know they weren't interested in recording his big band. (CBS had bought Rogers in April of that year.) Buddy's parting shot was, "If I'm not good enough for their records, then I'm not playing their drums." Off he went to Vox and then to Slingerland. (Rogers' other phenomenal endorser in the '60s and into the '70s was Louie Bellson, who was featured prominently with his "Twin Bass" setup.)

The rock acts of the 1960s also heavily endorsed Rogers—starting with the Dave Clark Five. Clark's first set actually had Ajax shells with Rogers hardware, and the double toms were each suspended on separate *Swiv-O-Matic* holders mounted close to the back hoop of the bass drum. (Ajax drums were distributed by Boosey and Hawkes, Rogers' English distributor.) Many rock players thought Rogers holders were the best, so *Swiv-O-Matic* units found their way onto the drums of other brands. Ringo, Ginger Baker, and Mitch Mitchell had them on Ludwig drums. Dennis Wilson had them on his Camcos. (Camco even installed Rogers hardware at their Oaklawn, Illinois factory.)

By the time of the 1964 catalog, Rogers produced the most expensive *everything*. Their snare drums (with their high-collared hoops), their *Swiv-O-Matic* hi-hats and pedals, and their holders always cost about 50% more than the competition's products. And the drums were heavy. The leg holders—called *Knobby* units—and the other metal parts made a Rogers floor tom considerably heavier than one from Ludwig or Slingerland. Rogers also used a five-ply shell while most others stayed at three plies.

In 1967, Rogers, by then under CBS ownership, released what I consider the most beautiful drum catalog ever made. It actually was prepared while Buddy was still in the fold, because there are two versions. One version has Buddy and Louie on the back cover; the other has a marching drum player next to Bellson. There are other minor differences on the first page of each of the two versions. This catalog shows Rogers in its glory days.

There are lots of Rogers drums to be had, so here are some things to look for to help you sort them out. All Grossman-era drums have stickers inside the shells that say: "Rogers, Cleveland, Ohio." (That's where they were warehoused and sold from.) After CBS bought the company in 1966 warehousing was moved to Dayton, Ohio, so Rogers drums from that year until 1969 have stickers that say Dayton. Remember, however, that *all* of these drums were made in the Covington, Ohio plant that was built in 1954 on Joe Thompson's property—so there is no difference in the quality of pre-CBS or post-CBS drums made in Ohio.

Cleveland-stickered drums have a flat gray primer on the inside of each shell (except for *Dyna-Sonics*, which have a

Swiv-O-Matic hardware was a major step forward in drum and cymbal mounting systems.

clear sealant). Dayton drums have a speckled gray finish, as do drums built in Fullerton, California (after CBS moved the company there in 1969). (The California operation got started as this book's timeline ends. I'm sure it was a very sad time in Ohio when Rogers production was moved to California. Most of the factory force chose to remain in Ohio. The Covington plant was eventually sold to a storm-window manufacturer.)

The easiest Rogers snare drum to find is the metal *Dyna-Sonic*—a beautiful, chrome-plated brass snare. The toughest model to find is the wood-shell *Dyna-Sonic*. That makes it extremely valuable. The 5x14 is rare, but the 6½x14 is even rarer. I've seen only four 5x14s in twenty-five years, and only one 6½x14. (And I bought all five drums!)

Here's a humorous bit of background to be aware of in case you're looking for a Rogers drum to match an existing set. Rogers bought most of their pearl sparkle covering materials from Rowland Plastics of Berlin, Connecticut. Rowland told Ben Strauss that most of their business came from eyeglass manufacturers. (Anyone out there ever see blue sparkle bifocals?) Ben was confounded by shade differences. At one time the factory had *nine* different shades of black diamond pearl alone. They had to keep them all separate until full sets were completed in order to avoid confusion and mis-matching. Complaining to Rowland didn't help, because they had all the eyeglass-frame business they needed and weren't really concerned with Rogers' problems.

So the next time the 9x13 you find doesn't quite match your snare drum, it may not be because one of them faded. It might be because the oculists of the 1960s were also pushing your color!

Snare Drums 1930s & '40s

Three Star
5x14, 6½x14
wood or metal shells
8 Gretsch *Broadkaster* (*Rocket*) lugs
Radio King strainer
double-flanged Gretsch hoops
pearl, chrome

Mercedes
5x14
wood shells
8 Gretsch *Broadkaster* lugs
Rogers (*Frank Wolf*) strainer
double-flanged Gretsch hoops
chrome, nickel, Klondyke gold plating
pearl, mahogany

Superior
5x14
beaded brass shell
double-flanged Gretsch hoops
chrome, nickel, Klondyke gold plating

Brighton
5x14 wood or metal shells
6½x14 metal shell
8 Gretsch *Broadkaster* lugs
two-hole *Premier* strainer
single-flanged hoops with clips
chrome, nickel, Klondyke gold plating
pearl, lacquer, mahogany, brass

Princeton
5x14
wood or metal shells
6 single-tension rods
simple strainer mounted on hoop
flat hoops with clips
mahogany, metal

Manville
16 thumb rods
Duplex strainer
mahogany with maple hoops

Sultan
6½x14, 7x14, 7x15
3-ply mahogany shell with wooden counterhoops
8 claws and rods
8 "Modernistic" lugs ("R" stamped on)
two-hole *Premier* strainer
chrome, nickel plating
mahogany, lacquer, pearl

Goodwill
5x14, 6½x14, 7x14, 8x14
wood or metal shells
8 "Modernistic" lugs
Radio King strainer
single-flanged hoops with clips
chrome, nickel plating
pearl, nickel, mahogany

Utility
brass or mahogany shells
6 "Modernistic" lugs
two-hole *Premier* strainer
flat hoops with clips
nickel plating

Bass Drums 1930s & '40s
(all have maple hoops)

Three Star Supreme
5-ply
tube lugs
separate- or single-tension
chrome, pearl

Aristocrat Separate Tension
same as *Three Star* except:
chrome, nickel, Klondyke gold plating
mahogany, lacquer

Aristocrat Single Tension
same as above but single-tension

Dictator
3-ply mahogany shell
single- or separate-tension
chrome, nickel, Klondyke gold plating
pearl, mahogany, lacquer

Commander
same as *Dictator* except center posts have no outside washers and shells have thinner plies

Corporal
2-ply shell
thumb rods instead of regular timpani rods
nickel plating only
mahogany, lacquer

Sentry
same as *Corporal* but without centers (studs) for rods

TOM-TOMS 1940s

Single-Tension Tunable:
Simple Lug
6½x10, 8x12, 9x13, 12x14, 16x16
wood or metal hoops
tacked bottom head
claws or clips
nickel or chrome plating
pearl or lacquer

Cast Lug
8x12, 9x13, 12x14, 16x16
"Modernistic" lugs
tacked bottom head
single-flanged hoops with clips
nickel or chrome plating
pearl or lacquer

Separate-Tension Tunable:
Simple Lug
same as single-tension but sizes are:
  8x12, 9x13, 12x14, 16x16
calf heads on both sides
T-rods or regular rods

Non-Tunable (Tacked Heads):
China Type
4x10, 5½x12, 9x13, 12x14, 16x16
Chinese red or other lacquer finish

SNARE DRUMS 1950s

Holiday
5x14, 6½x14
8 drawn-brass lugs
triple-flanged hoops
Orchestra model (*Premier*) strainer
chrome plating

Century
8x15
16 small drawn-brass lugs
Orchestra (Rogers) strainer
triple-flanged hoops
chrome plating
pearl, mahogany, lacquer

Mayfair
5x14, 6½x14
8 drawn-brass lugs
Orchestra strainer
triple-flanged hoops
chrome plating
lacquer only (blue/silver and black/gold)

Broadway
same as *Mayfair* except: 5x14
white lacquer only

Monitor
same as *Mayfair* except: mahogany only

Luxor
5x14 only
6 drawn-brass lugs
Orchestra strainer
triple-flanged hoops
chrome plating
blue/silver or black/gold

Broadway
same as *Luxor* but with pearl covering

Classmate
4x13 single-tension
single-flanged hoops with clips
  (clips on bottom are threaded)
lacquer or pearl

BASS DRUMS 1950s

Holiday
14x20, 14x22
separate-tension
drawn-brass lugs
chrome plating
pearl with pearl inlaid hoops

Spotlight
14x20 only
center-mounted drawn-brass lugs with separate tension
chrome plating
pearl with pearl inlaid hoops

Mayfair
14x22 only
center-mounted drawn-brass lugs with separate tension
chrome plating
pearl or black/gold or blue/silver, pearl inlaid hoops

Monitor
14x22, 14x24, 14x26, 14x28
single- or separate-tension center-mounted drawn-brass lugs
chrome plating
mahogany or pearl

Classmate
12x22
single-tension with centers (studs)
white lacquer, blue/silver, or black/gold

The Dyna-Sonic snare featured a "floating" snare frame that prevented choking.
Created in the early '60s, it's still a popular design today.

Tom-Toms 1950s

Holiday
8x12, 9x13:
initially small, then later large drawn-brass lugs
triple-flanged hoops
chrome plating
pearl

16x16 only:
triple-flanged hoops
initially, small drawn-brass lugs, then large lugs
choice of straight, flared, or wide-spread (*Knobby*) legs
pearl

Spotlight
8x12, 9x13
center-mounted drawn-brass lugs
triple-flanged hoops
pearl

Mayfair
same as *Spotlight* but 9x13 and 12x15
blue/silver or black/gold

Luxor
8x12 only
single head
small drawn-brass lugs
triple-flanged hoops
blue/silver, black/gold, white marine,
    or black diamond pearl

Snare Drums 1960s

Dyna-Sonic
5x14, 6½x14 (8x15 in wood only)
5-ply maple or brass shells (wood shell has reinforcing ring)
10 drawn-brass then *Beavertail* lugs
Swiv-O-Matic strainer
triple-flanged hoops
snare frame

Holiday
5x14, 6½x14
5-ply maple with maple reinforcing rings
8 drawn-brass lugs
triple-flanged hoops
pearl, lacquer, mahogany

Power Tone
replaces *Holiday*
5x14, 6½x14
brass shell or 5-ply maple shell with maple reinforcing rings
8 *Beavertail* lugs
triple-flanged hoops

Century
8x15 only
16 small drawn-brass, then *Beavertail* lugs
Swiv-O-Matic strainer
triple-flanged hoops
pearl, lacquer, mahogany

Tower
5x14, 6½x14
8 drawn-brass, then *Beavertail* lugs
Universal (*Orchestra*) strainer then *Sta-Tite* strainer
triple-flanged hoops
pearl, lacquer, mahogany

Luxor
same as *Tower* but 6 lugs

Student
same as *Luxor* except single-flanged hoops with clips

Classmate
4x13
single-tension, center studs
Universal strainer
flat hoops with clips
lacquer or mahogany

Banner
same as *Classmate* except 5x14
pearl, lacquer, mahogany

Bass Drums 1960s

Holiday
12x20, 14x20, 12x22, 14x22, 14x24, 14x26, 14x28
separate-tension drawn-brass, then *Beavertail* lugs
bow-tie T-rods, then *Dayton* design
pearl, lacquer, mahogany, with pearl inlaid hoops

Tower
14x20, 14x22, 14x24, 14x26, 14x28
separate-tension center drawn-brass, then *Beavertail* lugs
pearl, lacquer, mahogany, with pearl inlaid hoops

Concert
14x28, 14x30, 14x32, 16x30, 16x32
separate-tension drawn-brass, then *Beavertail* lugs
pearl, lacquer, mahogany, with pearl inlaid hoops

Mercury
14x20, 14x22, 14x24, 14x26, 14x28
center-mounted single-tension drawn-brass,
    then *Beavertail* lugs
pearl, lacquer, mahogany

Classmate
14x20 only
center studs
single-tension
lacquer only

By the mid-1960s, Rogers was making the most expensive and sought-after drums in America.

Tom-Toms 1960s
(5-ply maple with reinforcing rings)

Holiday
8x12, 9x13, 14x14, 14x16, 16x16
large drawn-brass, then small *Beavertail* lugs
triple-flanged hoops
floor toms: choice of straight, flared,
   or wide-spread (*Knobby*) legs
pearl, lacquer

Tower
8x12, 9x13, 12x15, 14x14 (straight or flared legs)
Separate-tension center-mounted drawn-brass,
   then *Beavertail* lugs
pearl, lacquer, then lacquer only

Luxor
8x12, 9x13
single-headed toms
pearl, lacquer

Finishes

'30s/'40s
white marine pearl, black diamond pearl, emerald pearl, gold sparkle, silver sparkle, green sparkle, mahogany, black duco, white duco

'50s
Scotch plaid, solid black, black and gold, blue and silver, Mardi Gras pearl, red sparkle, blue sparkle

'60s
wine red ripple, steel gray ripple, sky blue ripple, blue onyx, black onyx, pink champagne, red onyx, black strata*, pink strata*, blue strata*

* same finish as oyster pearl

Slingerland Drum Company

Legend states that Henry Hannon Slingerland was a riverboat gambler working the Mississippi River trade. In a poker match with H.H., as he was known, was a man low on funds but desperate to win. He was allowed to bet his business instead of cash. Suddenly Mr. Slingerland found himself the new owner of a mail-order company specializing in ukulele lessons. Out of that inauspicious beginning came one of the greatest drum companies ever to exist.

The fad of college boys strumming ukuleles while crooning love songs to coeds was soon replaced by interest in another instrument: the banjo. At first used for novelty acts, the banjo became a popular part of American culture—and Slingerland became a manufacturer. Since both banjos and drums required wood- and metal-working operations and both called for calfskin heads, it was logical for Slingerland to expand operations and make drums. The official name of the firm was "Slingerland Banjo & Drum Company," manufacturers of banjos, drums, and guitars.

H.H. Slingerland built his company in Chicago as a rival to Ludwig & Ludwig. Chicago was a natural choice because of the famous stockyards, which were absolutely critical as a source from which to meet the demand for calf and slunk heads. (See the chapter on drumheads for a complete description of both.)

Early Slingerland catalogs displayed solid-wood-shell and spun-metal-shell snare drums that used tube lugs similar to those of Ludwig & Ludwig. Slingerland drums are easy to identify from a distance because of the notable badge and strainer mechanism. From the 1920s until right after World War II, Slingerland's badge used a scalloped design that has been affectionately dubbed "The Cloud Badge." The strainer has also been renamed. Originally called the *Speedy Sure-Hold,* it later became the *Radio King, Krupa,* or *Three-Point* strainer.

Company literature states that Slingerland was founded in 1916, but the first documented Slingerland catalog was issued in 1928. It featured a picture of their *Artist* model snare drum in metal shells with the *Black Beauty* finish. Although Ludwig & Ludwig is the company widely recognized as the *Black Beauty*'s originator, it was really Slingerland that publicized the name. The L&L model was the *Deluxe* or *Standard* with *Deluxe* finish. I've thought of the irony of this situation many times.

The Slingerland *Black Beauty* had a one-piece brass shell covered in black nickel. The rods, clips, single-flanged hoops, tube lugs, strainer, and butt plate were finished in brass with a gold-tinted lacquer sprayed on. Slingerland used the term "art gold" for this process—which was the same process used by Leedy (nobby gold) and Ludwig & Ludwig (*Deluxe*). The lacquer would eventually wear off. If you find one, be careful when you clean it. *Never* use hot water. Instead, use a light oil like *3-In-1.*

It's thought that for a time Slingerland had drums built for them by other companies. Bill Ludwig, Jr. remembers that Slingerland bought Ludwig & Ludwig machinery when Conn moved the plant from Chicago to Elkhart, Indiana in the early '30s. That's another bit of irony: former Ludwig manufacturing equipment used against it by its arch rival.

Another story circulating through drum lore is that the father of rising drum sensation Gene Krupa was a big booster of his son's drumming. Since the Krupas were from Chicago, dad called Ludwig & Ludwig to get Gene a modern set. Ludwig couldn't help because the factory had been moved to Elkhart by Conn, and the Chicago office only handled sales to dealers. So, Mr. Krupa looked in the phone book and called the Slingerland Banjo Company—which also made drums.

H.H. saw his moment and sold the Krupas a set at dealer cost. From then and for almost forty years, Gene Krupa was the greatest drum salesman/ ambassador/cheerleader that Slingerland had.

At the time, Gene was getting major recognition with the Benny Goodman band, so H.H. listened when Gene offered a suggestion. Krupa was interested in tunable tom-toms. That may sound strange today, but as late as the mid-'30s most drum companies offered only non-tunable tom-toms—most of which were very shallow. Most used pigskin heads, which were thicker than calf and therefore easier to tack on. Calf heads needed to be tensioned frequently because of atmospheric changes. Eventually calf was placed on the top head and pigskin on the bottom. Slingerland was the first to put calf on both sides of the tom-toms and use timpani handles to tighten the heads. The earliest tunable toms came with tube lugs; cast lugs followed some years later. It was an incredibly important step in drum history. Remember it the next time you hear "Sing, Sing, Sing."

History has been kind to Slingerland. Their solid-shell *Radio King* series sits very high in drum hierarchy, and from the mid-'30s to the early '50s their catalogs show us that major players favored Slingerland more than any other brand. But quite frankly, I am not that impressed with Slingerland workmanship prior to the mid-'50s. The lugs are plated pot metal that pits, the *Radio King* and *Super Radio King* strainers are finicky, and the unfinished interiors of the drums look like the work of a freshman shop class. But Slingerland had an aura, a sound, a star, and a leader that combined to propel them forward. At one point, all drum companies had solid-shell snare drums. One by one they stopped making them until only Slingerland continued to market one. And the company turned that to an advantage.

H.H. Slingerland, Jr.—known as "Bud"—took over the company following his father's death in the '40s. Bud guided the company through the '50s and '60s before selling it to MacMillan & Co. in 1970, at which time he retired. He died in 1980 at the age of fifty-eight.

Bud Slingerland was a tough competitor. He and Bill Ludwig, Jr. were both second-generation warriors following in the footsteps of empire builders and battling each other for market share.

As I said earlier, in my opinion Slingerland made acceptable drums through the early '50s. But from the mid-'50s introduction of the *Sound King* lug until almost the end of its run as a major force in the drum industry, Slingerland built *great* musical instruments. By that point, the lugs were well-made and the woodwork was finished and professional-looking. The introduction of the *Zoomatic* and *Rapid* strainers also put an end to the awful ("clamshell") *Super* strainer.

In 1960, Slingerland moved to its new factory in Niles, Illinois, where it remained until the company ceased manufacturing in the early 1980s. (For a period in the mid-'60s, a second production facility was set up in Shelbyville, Tennessee. Those drums have maroon badges and the reinforcement hoops are oak.) In 1983, Fred Gretsch (a descendant of the founder of Gretsch Drums) bought the company and moved the machinery and parts to the Gretsch factory in South Carolina. His efforts to re-establish the line were not particularly successful, and in 1994 he sold Slingerland to the Gibson Guitar Company. It remains to be seen what the future will hold for this venerable name in American drum history.

SNARE DRUMS LATE 1920s

Artist Model
4x14, 5x14, 6½x14
solid-walnut or spun-brass shells
8 tube lugs with nickel or art gold plating
Speedy-Sure Hold (Krupa) strainer
single-flanged hoops with clips
all finishes

Professional Model
4x14, 5x14, 6½x14
solid-walnut, mahogany,
   or metal shells
8 tube lugs with nickel plating
Speedy-Sure Hold strainer
single-flanged hoops with clips
mahogany or walnut finishes
   (or all nickel if metal shell)

Universal Model
4x14, 5x14
solid-mahogany or metal shells
6 tube lugs with nickel plating
Junior snare throwoff
straight hoops with clips
mahogany finish (or all nickel
   if metal shell)

Also three thumb rod snares:
   3x13 to 5x15—the *Juvenile*,
   the *Tango* model, and the
   Thumb Rod model.

BASS DRUMS LATE 1920s
solid shells and laminated shells
   with single- and separate-
   tension from 12x26 to 18x34

solid shells available only
   in 14x26 and 14x28 sizes and
   finished in brown mahogany,
   black or white enamel,
   or in maple

only laminated drums covered in
pearl

A 1920s-era Slingerland Professional model snare drum

Gene Krupa (shown here circa 1937) may be credited with the development of tunable, double-headed tom-toms. He almost certainly is responsible for bringing Slingerland drums to the forefront of public attention.

FINISHES LATE 1920s

Drums
black diamond, black (ebony) enamel, gold sparkle, marine pearl, mahogany, maple (bass only), sea green, walnut, white enamel

Metal (shells and fittings)
nickel, art gold, or gold plating

SNARE DRUMS EARLY 1930s

DuAll
5x14, 6½x14
black metal engraved shell
   or solid-maple shell
10 tube lugs
DuAll strainer
single-flanged engraved top hoop,
   single-flanged bottom hoop
nickel, chrome, art gold fittings

Artist Model
4x14, 5x14, 6½x14
same as *DuAll* except:
   Three-Point (Krupa) strainer
   non-engraved top hoop

Professional Model
same as *Artist* except:
   8 tube lugs available with nickel plating
   no pearl finishes

Universal Model
same as *Professional* except:
   5x14 only
   6 tube lugs
   Shur-Hold strainer
   straight hoops
   nickel or white or black enamel

Broadcaster
1935 only
solid shell: walnut, mahogany, maple
8 streamlined lugs
Three-Point (Krupa) strainer
engraved hoops
this was the third "pre-*Radio King*"
   Radio King (solid shell)

Junior Snare Drums
5 available from 3x12 to 4x14

BASS DRUMS EARLY 1930s
5-ply *Artist* model in separate- or single-tension
   in sizes from 12x26 to 16x30
also available in 3-ply models from 12x26 to 18x34

FINISHES EARLY 1930s
All Drums
antique (blue/silver/black/gold), black diamond,
coral pearl, marine pearl, opal (peacock) pearl,
sea green pearl, sparkling gold, sparkling green,
sparkling red, sparkling silver

Metal Drums
chrome, nickel, art gold

SNARE DRUMS LATE 1930s
Radio King–Metal
6½x14
beaded shell
10 *Streamlined* lugs

Radio King–Wood
5x14, 6½x14
solid-wood shell
Krupa strainer with extension bridge
double-flanged hoops
engraved top hoop
nickel or chrome plating

(two screws hold each side of the *Radio King*'s bridges)

Gene Krupa Radio King
6½x14
8 lugs
the "Number One Drum"
   of the Slingerland line
originally offered only in marine pearl

Ben Pollack Radio King
same as *Krupa* model but
   with wooden hoops and claws

Bernie Mattison Radio King
same as *Krupa* model but
   only in 8x14 size

Band Master Radio King
same as *Mattison* but
   with wooden hoops and claws

Professional Model Radio King
same as early '30s

Universal Model Radio King
same as early '30s

Junior Model Radio King
5 available from 3x12 to 4x14

BASS DRUMS LATE 1930s
same as early '30s with the addition of
the *Universal* series—a 2-ply shell in
separate or single tension built in sizes
from 8x22 to 16x30

TOM-TOMS LATE 1930s
9x13, 12x14, 16x16
tunable on both heads or tunable on top with
   tacked pigskin on the bottom
top heads tensioned with timpani-handled rods
Streamlined or tube lugs
no legs available

FINISHES LATE 1930s
Drums
abalone pearl, antique (blue/black/gold/silver), black diamond pearl, peacock pearl, sea green pearl, sparkling gold,
sparkling green, sparkling red

Metal (shells and fittings)
chrome or nickel plating

SNARE DRUMS 1940s
(three screws hold each side of the *Radio King's* bridges)

Slingerland Radio King drums (such as this 1948 model)
enjoyed great popularity from the 1930s through the
1950s—and are among the most highly prized vintage
drums today.

H.H. Slingerland,
namesake of a major
American drum line

H.H. "Bud" Slingerland,
Jr. ran the company
from the late 1940s
until 1970.

In 1960 the Slingerland factory in Niles, Illinois was
claimed to be the "world's largest, most modern
drum plant."

Hollywood Ace
(*Maurice "Mo" Purtill*)
7x14, 8x14
double rows of *Super Streamlined*
   (aka *Beavertail*) lugs
Krupa strainer
nickel, chrome plating
pearl, duco

Gene Krupa
same as 1930s except: 7x14 and 8x14
   nickel, chrome plating
   all pearl finishes, duco

Buddy Rich
same as *Hollywood Ace* except:
   without extension bridges
   nickel, chrome plating

Ray McKinley
7x14, 8x14
similar to 1930s *Ben Pollack* but:
   counter-sunk claws holding
      wooden hoop
   bottom hoop is
      double-flanged metal
   nickel, chrome plating
   pearl, duco

Artist Model
6½x14
one-piece brass shell
16 super *Streamlined* lugs
no extension bridges
nickel, chrome plating

Super Radio King
7x14, 8x14
16 *Super Streamlined* lugs
Super strainer (clamshell)
no extension bridges
nickel, chrome plating
pearl, duco

Professional
brass—5x14, 6½x14
solid-wood—6½x14, 7x14
8 tube lugs
nickel-plated only
single-flanged hoops with clips
Krupa strainer

Universal
brass—5x14
solid-wood—5x14, 6½x14
6 tube lugs
Speedy Sure-Hold (4 hole) strainer
flat hoops with clips
mahogany on wood
white or black duco available on metal
nickel plating only

Continuation of the 5 *Junior* models

BASS DRUMS 1940s
(changes to 3-ply)
Radio King lugs on *Radio King* and *Artist* models
separate- or single-tension

Radio King
14x26, 14x28
pearl, duco
nickel, chrome plating

Artist Model
12x24, 16x36
antique, duco, mahogany, walnut

Universal Model
8x22 to 16x30: single- and separate-tension tube lugs
12x26 to 16x34: single-tension
mahogany or maple

TOM-TOMS 1940s
Tacked
6x10, 8x12, 9x13, 12x14
duco only

Radio Kings
7x11, 8x12, 9x13, 12x14, 14x16, 16x16
Streamlined or *Super Streamlined* lugs

A 1960s-vintage Buddy Rich Model kit, created at the peak of
Slingerland's quality and popularity

Single-Tension
same sizes
tunable top heads, tacked bottom heads
available in pearl, duco
nickel, chrome plating

FINISHES 1940s
sparkling gold, green, red, silver, black diamond pearl, white
marine pearl, antique (blue & silver, black & gold)

SNARE DRUMS LATE 1940s
Gene Krupa Radio King
adds 5½x14

Student Model Radio King
5½x14, 7x14
3-ply shell
Streamlined lugs
Krupa strainer
single-flanged hoops with clips
mahogany or lacquer
nickel plating

Concert King
6½x14, 6½x15, 8x15
3-ply shell
16 *Super Streamlined* lugs
Krupa strainer
double-flanged hoops
mahogany, lacquer, pearl

BeBop
4x13
8 *Streamlined* lugs
Krupa strainer
double-flanged hoops
nickel, chrome plating
pearl, duco

BASS DRUMS LATE 1940s
Radio King
14x20 and 14x22 available

TOM-TOMS LATE 1940s
add 16x18, 16x20, 20x20
double-flanged hoops
both cradles and legs available for floor toms
single-headed toms available: 7x10, 8x12

FINISHES LATE 1940s
add blue sparkle, knotty pine lacquer, simulated marble

MID-'50s
introduction of the *Sound King* lug

add *Special Student* drum:
   3-ply laminated shell
   6 lugs
   Krupa strainer
   flat hoops withclips

LATE '50s/EARLY '60s
introduction of *Stick Saver* hoops
all hardware is chrome-plated

SNARE DRUMS '50s/'60s
Super Gene Krupa Snare Drum
(new name for *Super Radio King*)
5½x13, 5½x14: 8 *Sound King* lugs
7x14, 8x16: 16 *Sound King* lugs (double row)

Artist Model
(replaces *Super Radio King)*
solid shell
8 lugs
Zoomatic strainer

Gene Krupa Model
same except hoops (non-engraved stick savers)

Hollywood Ace
8 *Sound King* lugs
Rapid strainer

Festival
brass shell
8 lugs
Rapid strainer
chrome plating

Student Aluminum
8 lugs
Rapid strainer

Concert King
same except:
   Stick Saver hoops
   later with *Rapid* strainer

Deluxe Concert King
same as *Concert King* except: *Zoomatic* strainer

Student Model
(no longer says *Radio King*)
same except:
   Rapid strainer
   can be pearl

Deluxe Student
same as Student except: *Stick Saver* hoops

Special Student Drum
Rapid strainer
6 lugs
flat hoops with clips

Brass Shell
lacquered brass shell
8 *Sound King* lugs
Krupa strainer
Rapid strainer available

Concert Hall
$6\frac{1}{2}$x14, $6\frac{1}{2}$x15, 8x15
8 lugs
Rapid strainer
mahogany or lacquer

Gene Krupa Sound King
5x14, $6\frac{1}{2}$x14
brass shell
8 or 10 lugs
Zoomatic strainer
brass, chrome plating

Radio King
5x14, $6\frac{1}{2}$x14
brass shell
8 or 10 lugs
Krupa strainer (one screw into bridge)
brass, chrome plating

Super Sound King
5x14, $6\frac{1}{2}$x14
brass shell
8 or 10 lugs
dual *Super* strainer
brass, chrome plating

BASS DRUMS '50/'60s
add 12x20, 12x22, 12x24, 14x28, 16x16
new T-rods and claws
Radio King name disappears

TOM-TOMS '50s/'60s
18x20 is now largest size
single-headed toms: 9x10, 9x13, 14x16 available
Standard model: center-mounted *Sound King* lug, with
   8x12, 9x13, 12x15, 14x14, 14x16 available
pearl, lacquer

FINISHES '50s/'60s
add:
light blue pearl, oyster pink, blue ripple pearl, capri pearl, gold veiled ebony pearl, black sparkle, pink champagne, pink sparkle, peacock sparkle, fiesta pearl, Mardi gras pearl, silver veil, maroon and gold lacquer, green and gold lacquer, blue agate (1969), gray agate (1969), red tiger (1969), white tiger (1969), yellow tiger (1969), blue satin flame (1969), gold satin flame (1969), red satin flame (1969), tangerine satin flame (1969), lavender satin flame (1969), white satin flame (1969), green satin flame (1969), black beauty pearl (solid black)

Chapter 13

WFL Drum Company

Drums & Drummers' Instruments • World's Largest Drum Manufacturer

In 1936, William F. Ludwig, Sr. decided to leave Ludwig & Ludwig, which was then a division of the Conn organization. Stories handed down tell of infighting with the Leedy side of the house—particularly with George Way. Conn management considered Leedy the "top dog" while Ludwig was consigned to second place. No wonder someone with talent and drive decided to try again.

So, at the age of fifty-eight William F. Ludwig, Sr. left what had been his company—with only his Conn stock as a negotiable asset. That stock had been worth a million dollars when he signed over Ludwig & Ludwig in 1930. But with the depressed world conditions in 1936, it was reduced in value by 90%. With that one hundred thousand dollars Bill and Elsa Ludwig—and their children, Betty and Bill Junior—left Elkhart and moved home to Chicago.

Imagine starting over at fifty-eight with only 10% of what you'd worked thirty years to get. Was he brave, or crazy—or both? Bill Junior once told me his dad *was* a little crazy—though in a nice way. He loved building drums. He worked six days a week, couldn't wait to get to the factory, and hated to go home. Sundays were reserved for dinners with visiting professionals and for drum talk. And this went on until he was ninety-four.

Bill Senior bought a building on Damen Avenue (which would serve the drumming community for almost the next fifty years). With a handful of employees, he launched the William F. Ludwig Drum Company. He also advertised that he was no longer affiliated with Ludwig & Ludwig—which did not amuse Conn's management. Legal action was threatened. After all, Conn reasoned, they had bought the Ludwig name. Whether it was used singularly or not, it was still a trade name and it was theirs.

A brainstorming session took place at the new company. To survive, they had to let customers know that Bill Ludwig, Sr. had his own company again. It was not the *same* company, but it *was* the same Bill Ludwig. They figured that though Conn had taken his name away, they couldn't take away his initials. So the upstart William F. Ludwig Drum Company became the WFL Drum Company. (The company retained that name until the Ludwigs were able to buy half of the Conn drum division in 1955. The details of that transaction can be found in the chapter on Leedy & Ludwig.)

In 1909, Bill Ludwig, Sr. had hand-carved a prototype pedal that was produced in steel for other drummers. That pedal had started an empire of manufacturing. In 1937, history repeated itself. A WFL employee designed a pedal that featured compression springs housed in the pedal's vertical supports. WFL unveiled the *Speed King*—the most widely sold pedal in history—and Bill Ludwig was officially back in business. (An original *Speed King,* by the way, does not look exactly like the more universally recognized model released in the early 1950s. The original *Speed King* was called the *Twin Spring Speed King* and had a narrower footboard—but still had a reversible heel plate.)

Bill Ludwig pulled together a great front-office team to go head-to-head with the big companies. From L&S in Indianapolis came former Leedy engineer Cecil Strupe as general manager. Palmer Laycock, another former Leedy Indianapolis executive, became sales manager, and William F. Ludwig, Jr. signed on as advertising manager. Dad, son, and the other executives geared up for drum wars. Little WFL presented exciting new products to the public in very rapid succession. After the *Speed King* pedal came a double-snare-mechanism snare drum called the *Twin Strainer* (as well as the *Ray Bauduc* model and the *World's Fair* model).

The *Twin Strainer* model was revolutionary. The two thin strainers sat side-by-side. One set controlled wire snares; the other activated and released silk wire-wound snares. A player could get response even at pianissimo.

Another notable improvement was the triple-flanged design of the WFL drum hoops. Such hoops are commonplace on today's models, but back then they were revolutionary. A big complaint about the then-common double-flanged hoops was stick breakage. It went like this: "If wood hits metal, metal wins." Cecil Strupe used pliers to bend down the top of a double-flanged hoop, thus creating a

Since he couldn't use his own name for his new company, William F. Ludwig used his initials—and in 1936 the WFL Drum Company was born.

rounder, more "stick-friendly" edge. The sales staff knew it was a breakthrough, and they went to work advertising that WFL had an exclusive. And it stayed that way for twenty years. The company also released new pedal timpani and a "host of other new and practical percussive ideas."

WFL started business with three lugs. The first was a tube lug resurrected from the earlier Ludwig & Ludwig design. Secondly, a beautiful cast lug was created by Strupe and christened the *Imperial*. (The same name is used to describe the lug on a modern Ludwig *Supraphonic,* but the designs are different.) The last lug was a pressed-steel piece called the *Zephyr*. (The name was popular at that time because of a streamlined train and a new, low-cost Lincoln automobile that both used the Zephyr name. Each symbolized the "modern look.")

Personally speaking, I think the *Zephyr* lug is extremely unattractive, but I know the reason for it. Mrs. Ludwig was the bank, and she was trying to stretch the stock-redemption money as far as possible. The *Zephyr* lug was cheap to make, while the *Imperial* was made from a more costly sand casting.

During World War II, a skeleton crew ran the company while Bill Junior went into the Navy and Bill Senior and Cecil Strupe went to Cleveland to help run a factory converted to the manufacture of war material. WFL subsisted by making the *Victorious* line of drums. Strupe designed them with wooden lugs and an internal tensioning device: A mid-shell drum rod could be tightened to expand a wooden bow. That action raised rings to tighten each head. The line was

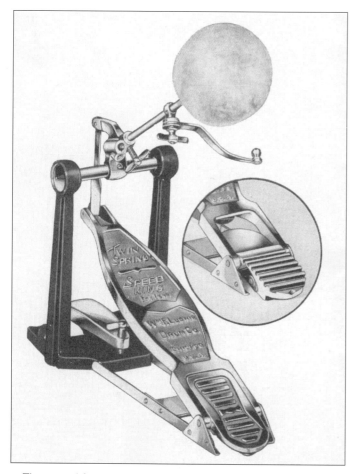

The famous Ludwig factory on Damen Avenue in Chicago served the drummers of America for almost fifty years.

a total failure, and was a major reason for Strupe's departure from WFL.

After the war, the Ludwigs were reunited (without Strupe) and began a meteoric rise. In the late '40s the *Classic* lug was introduced, and a drum legend was signed as an endorser. He was, of course, Buddy Rich. Although Buddy often fought with Bill Junior (who was his contemporary in age), he had great respect for Bill Senior. Buddy had played original Ludwig & Ludwig drums until his big band career started, at which time he switched to Slingerland with the help of Bill Mather. (See the chapter on Slingerland.) But Bill Junior pitched Buddy with just the right slant: No matter how much attention Buddy got in the music world, he would always be second at Slingerland. There was no room for Buddy as the "top guy" as long as Slingerland had Gene Krupa. So for a promise of three sets a year and advertising, Rich signed on with WFL. (That relationship lasted until 1960, and the breakup is documented in the chapters on Ludwig and Rogers.)

In 1949, the *Buddy Rich Super Classic* set—$6\frac{1}{2}$x14 snare, 9x13 and 16x16 toms, and a 14x26 bass drum with hi-hat, pedal, snare stand, two cymbal holders, sticks, brushes, cowbell, holder, and muffler—sold for less than $400. You can almost get a nice snare drum for that price now.

In 1954, C.G. Conn Ltd. decided to suspend drum operations in favor of the manufacturing of electronic organs. This was the same company that bought Leedy in 1929 for $950,000 in cash and later bought Ludwig & Ludwig for one million dollars in stock. After selling their inventory of finished products, Conn arranged a deal with Bill Ludwig, Jr.: Conn would sell Leedy & Ludwig for $180,000.

WFL didn't *need* to make a deal, but it was an opportunity for the Ludwigs to get their name again. (Imagine competing with a company that carried your name—after you had built it—and then having the chance to buy it back at a bargain price.) Even so, Bill Ludwig, Jr. must have been the consummate salesman, because he convinced his mortal enemy, Bud Slingerland, to put up half of the purchase price for Leedy & Ludwig. Leedy, with all its dies and patents, would go to Slingerland; WFL would get all the Ludwig & Ludwig assets. (For more details see chapter 6.)

The WFL logo was selected because Bill Ludwig, Sr. liked a certain brand of motor oil that used the Pennsylvania Keystone on the label of the can. The first version read: "Wm. F. Ludwig Drum Company." After Conn threatened legal action, the logo was changed to WFL. The keystone was readily distinctive when compared to the oval of Ludwig & Ludwig, the scalloped "cloud" badge of Slingerland, and the decorative rectangle of Leedy.

In the 1956 catalog, both the Ludwig and the WFL names and logos were used. *Speed King* pedals, hi-hats, and snare stands had WFL stamped on them, and it was years after the name change before the factory finally sold the last of them.

In 1959-60, the firm finally changed badges to a larger keystone that carried the Ludwig name. The design had the logo in a blue oval, and has been dubbed the "Transition Badge." (For more discussion, please see the Ludwig chapter.)

The original Speed King pedal was a WFL product released in 1937. It pre-dated the more familiar version we know today, which was introduced in 1950.

Snare Drums 1930s/'40s

Twin Strainer
(aka *Dixie Swing*)(*World's Fair* if *Zephyr* lugs)
5x14, 7x14
3-ply mahogany
8 *Imperial* or *Zephyr* lugs
two versions of the strainer—earlier has straight arms,
   later has slightly curved arms. Second is more collectible.
triple-flanged hoops or wooden hoops
   with studs through inlay
chrome or nickel plating
pearl only
World's Fair not available with wooden hoops

Hollywood Swing
same as *World's Fair* with the following exceptions:
   also available in 15"
   metal-shell model available
   wooden counterhoops available
   chrome or nickel plating
   lacquer finish available as well as pearl

All American Swing
(aka *Single Strainer Dixieland* model)
same as *Hollywood Swing* except:
   with a single strainer

Concert
7x15
metal or mahogany shells
8 *Zephyr* lugs
triple-flanged hoops
chrome or nickel plating

Victor
(aka *Imperial Double-Flanged
   Swingster*)
7x14, 7x15
metal or mahogany shells
8 tube lugs
Ideal (*P33*) strainer
flat hoops with clips
(*Imperial* model also in 5x14 and
   used single strainer, not *Ideal*)

Paramount
5x14, 7x14
metal or mahogany shells
8 *Zephyr* lugs
lacquer, mahogany

Ideal
5x14
metal or mahogany shells
6 tube lugs and clips
flat hoops
Ideal strainer

There were also two low-end snares:
the *Ideal*, which featured 6 tube lugs on
a metal or mahogany shell with *Ideal*
strainer, and the *Juniorette*, which featured a 3½x13 mahogany drum with
straight hoops and 6 thumb rods.

The earliest WFL badges actually read
"Wm. F. Ludwig Drum Company"—until the
Conn company threatened legal action over
the Ludwig name.

The company dropped the name, but kept
the initials and the distinctive "Keystone"
badge shape.

Bass Drums 1930s/'40s

Imperial
3-ply mahogany with maple reinforcing hoops
   and maple counterhoops
Imperial lugs center-mounted with separate-tension
chrome, nickel plating
pearl, lacquer

Zephyr
same as *Imperial* model but with *Zephyr* lugs

Zephyr Single-Tension
same as *Zephyr* but with single-tension
long tension rods run through "empty" *Zephyr* lug
   into threaded claw
chrome or nickel plating
mahogany, black or white lacquer

Separate-Tension Tubular
tube lugs
chrome, nickel plating
pearl, mahogany

Standard
single-tension with center supports
long tension rods run through stud into threaded claws
mahogany or lacquer

Tom-Toms 1930s/'40s

Single-Tension
7x11, 8x12, 9x13, 12x14, 14x16
pigskin bottom heads (tacked)
small tom-tom lug (shaped like plier jaws)
   with threaded middle section—
   used with rods through clips
chrome or nickel plating
pearl or lacquer

Separate-Tension
same sizes and finishes as single-tension
initially center-mounted *Zephyr* lugs
   (some drums have *Imperial* lugs)
   tunable from both sides, separate
   Zephyr lugs by late '30s
(some non-tunable drums were made with
   pigskin heads tacked on both sides)

Finishes 1930s/'40s
white marine and black diamond, sparkling
silver, gold, red, green, blue and silver,
blue and gold, black and gold

Snare Drums Late 1940s/'50s

Buddy Rich Super Classic
5½x14
3-ply mahogany with maple glue rings
8 *Classic* lugs
Classic strainer
triple-flanged hoops
chrome or nickel plating
pearl, lacquer

Concert Model
6½x14
3-ply mahogany with maple glue rings
16 small *Classic* lugs
Classic strainer
triple-flanged hoops
chrome or nickel plating
pearl, lacquer, mahogany

Ray McKinley Super Classic
6½x14
same as *Concert* model but not available in mahogany

Concert Model
6½x14, 8x15
3-ply mahogany with maple glue rings
8 *Classic* lugs
P83 (*Concert*) strainer
triple-flanged hoops
chrome or nickel plating
pearl, lacquer, mahogany

Supreme Concert
6½x14
same as *Concert* model but with 6 *Classic* lugs
nickel plating only
mahogany or lacquer

Buddy Rich Be-Bop
3x13 (4x14 later called *Compacto*)
6 *Piccolo* lugs (4x14 used 8 *Piccolo* lugs)
Piccolo strainer
triple-flanged hoops
chrome plating only
pearl only

All Metal
6½x14
6 *Classic* lugs
P83 strainer
triple-flanged hoops
nickel plating only

Classic Porto Pak
5½x13
6 *Classic* lugs
Classic strainer
triple-flanged hoops
chrome or nickel plating
pearl only

Super Porto Pak
same as *Classic* except:
   with *P83* strainer

Festival Model School Concert
6½x14, 6½x15, 8x15
16 small *Classic* lugs
P83 strainer
triple-flanged hoops
chrome or nickel plating
mahogany, pearl, lacquer

Swingster Dance Model
5½x14
8 *Classic* lugs
P83 strainer
triple-flanged hoops
chrome or nickel plating
pearl or lacquer

BASS DRUMS
LATE 1940s/'50s

Super Classic
14x20, 14x22, 14x24, 14x26
3-ply mahogany
separate-tension *Classic* lugs
chrome or nickel plating
pearl, mahogany, lacquer

Super Classic School Model
14x28, 14x30, 16x32, 16x34, 16x36
same as *Super Classic*

Club Date
same as *Super Classic* but with center-mounted *Classic* lugs

Concert Bass
14x22, 14x24, 14x28, 14x30, 16x32, 16x34, 16x36
separate-tension center-mounted *Classic* lugs
chrome or nickel plating
mahogany, pearl, lacquer

Standard Bass
14x22, 14x24, 14x28
single-tension (center stud)
chrome or nickel plating
pearl, lacquer, mahogany

TOM-TOMS
LATE 1940s/'50s

Super Classic
8x12, 9x13, 12x14, 16x16, 16x18, 18x20
separate-tension *Classic* lugs
triple-flanged hoops
chrome or nickel plating
pearl, lacquer

Club Date
initially only in 9x13 and 12x15
separate-tension center-mounted *Classic* lugs
initially only available in lacquer

Chapter 14

George Way

George Way was a pioneer—a drummer, a retailer, a salesman, a designer, an advertiser, a cheerleader, and—according to those who knew him—a pleasant and likable man. It was his design that brought us the self-aligning lug and the look that today identifies Drum Workshop.

Way joined the Leedy Manufacturing company in 1921 as sales manager. Previously he had co-owned a retail store in Alberta known as the Advance Drum Company. Like some drumshops today, Advance made a few products themselves. The store was also the Canadian outlet for Leedy merchandise. I'm sure George sold Leedys with enough enthusiasm—and overwhelmed them with enough drawings and ideas—to get noticed. (My friend Rob Cook has published an excellent source called *George Way's Little Black Book* in which Way's ideas, designs, and a lifetime of contacts are listed. It is a must for collectors and refinishers.)

After thirty years of working for Leedy, Slingerland, Leedy & Ludwig, and Rogers, George Way found himself self-employed. He became a manufacturer's representative for Zildjian, Rogers, Amrawco, Evans, and a host of other companies. When the Conn organization sold the assets of its Leedy & Ludwig drum division in 1955 (see chapters 6 and 13), George Way leased the plant that Conn had used for Leedy & Ludwig production: the Buescher Building in Elkhart, Indiana.

By 1957 George was producing his own line of drums. They featured 3-ply shells from Jasper, Indiana—just like the ones Leedy, Ludwig & Ludwig, and Leedy & Ludwig had used. The shells were sealed with white lacquer, and the hoops were just like Leedy's (except that they had a slight triple flange). The big difference was Way's lug design. George called it

the *Turret,* and later it was known as the *Aristocrat.* Today, we simply call it the round lug. Later, he developed the *Tuxedo* model lug for use on less-expensive drum models.

I've heard stories about how Way came up with the round lug design. One was that he stacked the lids of jars, another was that he had a friend who had surplus horn parts that were fashioned into lugs. My unscientific guess is that he doodled the lug long before his drum company existed. In the '30s, Leedy used a half-moon lug on single-tension bass drums. A Way lug looked just like two of those lugs pushed together. All of the early lugs were for snare drums (because that's what Way built initially), so a special plug was inserted into the bottom opening of the lug for use on tom-toms, bass drums, or deep snare drums requiring two rows of lugs.

When the snare drums first appeared in 1957, George called them the *Paramount* models. But soon after, he used the name *Aristocrat.* The *Aristocrat* bass drum lugs sat on top of a chrome-plated O-ring. That lifted the lug to the height necessary to receive the T-handle.

It's very interesting to examine George Way drum parts (like floor-tom legs and their brackets or bass-drum claws and T-rods) and see the Leedy influence. And when you read the copy in the George Way catalog, you can be sure you are reading the work of the man who wrote the *Leedy Drum Topics* and the description for almost everything Leedy ever sold to the public.

From 1957 to 1961, the Way company hung on. George and a few ex-Conn employees, notably George Lewan, built their drums and sold them—along with products from other companies—to music stores across the country. No one had more contacts in the drum business than George Way. One of those contacts was John Rochon, president of Camco. Originally known as the Camco Drum

George Way in 1935, flanked by the Green brothers
(major music retailers of the period).

Courtesy Rob Cook

Accessory Company, Camco supplied George Way with pedals and stands. But in 1961 John Rochon supplied George with a pink slip when he bought controlling interest in the company and moved production to Oaklawn, Illinois. The "new" Camco drums retained the look of the George Way models, along with the *Aristocrat* name. The exception was the badge design. The George Way badge had a winged design in brass with black enamel. The Camco badge had the same shape, but was colored white.

After he lost his company to Camco, George Way went to work for Rogers, where he was given an easy task: He was picked to test *Dyna-Sonics*. But George drove them crazy

The flyer for the 1957 George Way Paramount snare drum illustrates the distinctive, round Aristocrat lug.

with his ideas. Although some may have had merit, one was to bring back hoop-mounted tom-tom holders. Imagine arguing that point with the company that had just designed the *Swiv-O-Matic* holder, arguably the best-engineered system of its day. George once again became unemployed, so he returned to Elkhart and created the GHW Company. (Knowing he could not use his name since Camco owned it, Way imitated the WFL move initiated in 1936 by William F. Ludwig, Sr.) As a manufacturer's rep George sold hundreds of items. Understandably, none of those were products manufactured by Camco.

SNARE DRUMS

Aristocrat
5½x14, 6½x14, 8x15
8 *Aristocrat* lugs (deep snares later used 16 lugs in a double row)
Precision strainer
triple-flanged hoops
chrome plating
pearl, lacquer, mahogany

Spartan
5½x14, 6½x14, 8x15
Precision strainer
single-flanged hoops with clips
chrome plating
pearl, lacquer, mahogany

BASS DRUMS

Aristocrat
14x22, 14x24
inlaid hoops
chrome plating
pearl, lacquer

Spartan
14x22, 14x24
inlaid hoops
chrome plating
pearl, lacquer

TOM-TOMS

Aristocrat
8x12, 9x13, 16x16
triple-flanged hoops
chrome plating
pearl, lacquer

Spartan
same sizes as *Aristocrats*
center-mounted *Aristocrat* lugs
single-flanged hoops with clips
chrome plating
pearl, lacquer

FINISHES
white marine pearl, black diamond, gold sparkle, blue sparkle, red sparkle, blue and silver lacquer, black and gold lacquer, and any special-order lacquer

The George Way badge had a winged shape, in brass with black enamel. (Camco badges were similar in shape, but were colored white.)

Chapter 15

Walberg & Auge

Walberg & Auge is probably the biggest unknown name in the history of twentieth-century American percussion. The catalogs of almost every manufacturer featured products built by this Worcester, Massachusetts company, but most of us never put together the clues.

In reality, no American company made all of its hardware. Lug casings, pedal parts, stands, etc. were "farmed out." Walberg & Auge, W&A, or just Walberg, as it is sometimes known, was a music store that became a manufacturer. Drums were made before 1910, but that eventually gave way to hardware manufacturing with only occasional drum output.

The story goes that Barney Walberg, president of the company, created the first hi-hat by modifying a low-boy. (A low-boy was a pedal-operated mechanism that brought two cymbals together. The mechanism sat low to the ground, hence the name.) Walberg fitted a low-boy with a long tube to elevate the cymbals, and the modern hi-hat was born.

Every company bought the Walberg hi-hats—generally in nickel plating and with variations only in the footboard. The typical model name used for W&A products was *Perfection,* so the *Perfection* hi-hat was shown in a number of catalogs. (Look for a model with a "skeleton" footboard.)

The really important W&A product, in my opinion, was the shell-mount tom-tom holder that eventually came to be used by all the companies. Prior to the late 1930s most tom-toms had "link" holders that connected to bass drum hoops, to rails mounted on the shell of the bass drum, or to consoles. Some time in the late '30s a New York Slingerland dealer named Bill Mather designed a new type of mount, and Walberg built it. The mount employed a diamond-shaped metal plate bolted to the ride tom. Into a raised section on this plate fit a spoon-shaped rod. The other end of the rod slid into a tilting mechanism that was fastened to a short rail section bolted to the bass drum shell.

At first only Slingerland had the Mather mount, which they dubbed the *Ray McKinley* Shell Mount Holder. But Walberg eventually sold it to all the other companies, who one by one either copied it or switched to an updated holder. Gretsch was the last company to stop using the shell-mount system.

After Barney Walberg died, his nephew Clarence ran the company.

Ben Strauss of Rogers remembers that Clarence had his office near an elevator. When Ben would call Clarence to order stands, Clarence would yell down the shaft to his chief engineer, "Ben's on the phone. How many *Buck Rogers* stands do we have?" Because W&A sold hardware to everyone, it was a constant battle for each company to get what it needed.

Rogers let Walberg make the first year's production of *Swiv-O-Matic* hi-hats, but moved the production in-house for the obvious "constant battle" reason.

My experience is that W&A plating is terrible; it's mostly nickel, although there are chrome parts as well. Still, no history of American percussion could be complete without Walberg & Auge, the "Perfection" people.

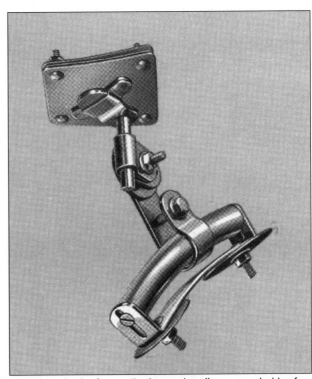

W&A made the famous "rail consolette" tom-tom holder for virtually every drum company from the late '30s on. Gretsch was the last one to stop using it, in the early '70s.

Chapter 16

Honorable Mention

I have created this category because a number of historic instrument manufacturers deserve special attention. I have listed eight such companies, each of which developed at least one product that made an impression on the public. We may never know exact sales numbers, because most companies did not record them. We can only react to the demand for them (as in the Billy Gladstones), remember the novelty (as in the Flat Jacks), or watch an idea tried again by another manufacturer (as in Frank Wolf or Zickos).

BARRY DRUM MANUFACTURING CO.
Manufacturers of Modern Drums for the Progressive Player

In 1919 a man named W.A. Barry built aluminum-shell drums in Philadelphia. His snare drums were die-cast in one piece and were finished with clear or tinted lacquer. The professional model had twelve lugs, which were tubes with a circular stud in the middle. There were vent holes between every lug (except for the section that held the strainer). The company also built wood-shell drums.

But Barry's real claim to fame was their collapsible bass drum. Since bass drums were normally 28" in diameter and streetcars were the primary means of transportation, our drumming forefathers faced dilemmas. (Think about lugging today's gear in fiber cases and riding a bus!) Barry's solution was a bass drum that could be reduced in size to fit in a special oval drum case that was pointed at each side like a ship's bow.

The owner had only to loosen and remove the tension rods, then push the drum together at its two hinge points. The 28" drum became a folded elliptical package that weighed $12\frac{1}{2}$ pounds. The company recommended the purchase of the *Companion* snare drum, a 3x13 that could fit in the case as well. Since most drums used 14" snares and needed a snare stand, too, Barry was glad to comply and illustrated a man holding all his gear in two easy-to-carry cases. (I wonder how he held onto the streetcar handle.)

Barry sold Ludwig & Ludwig traps and pedals as well as the Leedy *Fraserette* pedal. But the catalog space is really taken up by the drum information.

The Barry snare strainer (in nickel or gold plating) has a round center section. Through this circle passes a thumb screw for tightening the snares. The jaws, at the bottom of the thumb screw, have twelve round openings for wire or gut snares. The words "Barry" and "Pat. APD" are stamped on the round center section. A throwoff lever that folds down on the center section with a small handle facing to the right was the only model available.

I have only seen three Barry drums, and I'm struck with the idea that they were a regional company whose products were centered in the Northeast. I don't think that aluminum surfaced again as a shell material until Ludwig, Gretsch, and Slingerland introduced student-line snare drums made of aluminum in the 1960s.

The Barry collapsible bass drum

BILLY GLADSTONE

Romanian-born William Goldstein came to the United States in 1903 at age eleven. An immigration officer misheard his name, and from that day forward he became William Gladstone.

Billy Gladstone was both a talented drummer and a gifted inventor. He first gained notoriety as a pit drummer (and Leedy endorser) at the Capitol Theater in New York City. As his

Billy Gladstone in 1941

drumming fame grew over the years, so did his reputation for original design work. For example, the 1939 Gretsch catalog featured a remote hi-hat that was one of Billy's ideas. (Gretsch was the company whose products he used after leaving Leedy.)

Billy left the Capitol Theater to become the drummer at Radio City Music Hall, and a number of his inventions came about because of the cramped space in the orchestra pit. The most famous of these was his snare drum. Before World War II, Gretsch made two models called the Gretsch *Gladstones* (which are detailed in chapter 3). In the early '50s, Billy introduced his own Billy Gladstone drums. Drum historians figure that there were about fifty of these treasures made—four of them as part of drumsets. Billy's aide in the assembly of his drums was Charles Cordes. Construction took place inside Billy's one-room apartment in Manhattan. (And you thought *your* room was messy!)

A Billy Gladstone drum has a Gretsch shell (3-ply maple) with tube lugs connected in two places to the drum. The strainer, muffler, and hoops resemble those from earlier Gretsch *Gladstones,* but with minor differences. The drums were typically not pearl-covered due to Billy's aversion to coverings. The sizes were 6x14 and 7x14 and most were finished in either birds-eye maple or white, black, or gold lacquer. Metalwork was either chrome- or gold-plated. Each "BG" has a metal plate (with a finish that matches the hoops) that identifies the original owner.

When new, Billy Gladstone drums ranged from $250 to $350 in price. Near our publication date, one sold for $4,000. That's 1,143% growth in forty years. Not a bad way for an immigrant to be remembered. Only Ludwig & Ludwig *Black Beauties* have outpaced Billy Gladstones in appreciation.

Today a Gladstone replica snare drum is made in New York by Lang Percussion for the same price as many other high-end snare drums. Billy's not there to direct things, but Morris Lang builds a superb product. And he will allow you to have it pearl-covered if you'd like.

Billy invented a cable remote hi-hat featured in the 1939 Gretsch catalog.

DUPLEX MANUFACTURING COMPANY
Drum Construction At Its Best
Ultra-Fine Drums For The Modern Drummer

Duplex Manufacturing was started in St. Louis, Missouri by Emil Boulanger in the 1890s. The name is still used by Grossman Music of Cleveland (former owner of the Rogers Drum Company) as a brand name for snares and other percussion items. In the 60s, the Rogers factory actually built drums with the Duplex name. They had 5-ply shells, just like Rogers drums, but they had their own distinctive lug and holder design. From a distance they appear dissimilar to Rogers drums, but up close you can see the same "bow tie" tension rods and the same large-particle sparkles and pearl patterns/ shades. So those 1960s Duplex drums were really cousins of Rogers.

I can track the history of the original independent Duplex company to World War II, but

The Duplex badge

I'm not sure what happened then. I have read that Duplex claimed to be the first manufacturer to introduce separate-tension drums. Their version passed a thin tube through a center stud attached to the drum shell. Into each end of that tube small drum rods were tightened to tension the heads.

I've seen three Duplex snare drums—and pictures of a few more. The standouts have been the late-'30s products, which have a look all their own. One of those is a drum I own that is known as the *Spirit Of St. Louis.* The heads are 13" in diameter, but the body of the drum is 15". The 8"-deep shell is metal—riveted at the seam and covered in white marine pearl. Inside the shell are eight tube lugs.

The late-'30s-vintage Duplex Spirit Of St. Louis snare drum features a design strikingly like that utilized by Peavey's mid-'90s snares.

The tension rods pass through double-flanged hoops and into 15" aluminum rings that rest on the metal shell. Duplex called the interior of the shell the "Tone Chamber" and described the model as "America's Finest Drum." Judged by conventional designs, however, the drum looks strange. A 6½"-deep version also exists, as does a 5" brass-shell drum known as the *Standard Orchestra Model.* The latter drum has a 14 ½" tone chamber and the same 13" head. Duplex made tom-toms and bass drums with the same unusual design as the orchestra snares, but they also made conventional snares and basses. (From my research, I could not find "normal" tom-toms.)

The Duplex strainer was a very simple unit patented in 1914. Shaped like an upside down letter "T" with a small lever below the top-mounted tension knob, it can be found in other catalogs: Slingerland used it, Rogers used it, and a little known company called Novack used it. (Just to be fair, Duplex advertised products from Leedy, Ludwig & Ludwig, and Deagan in *their* catalog.)

If I were a betting man, I would say that the world passed Duplex by. Depending on your perspective, their look is very much old-fashioned…or bizarre. On the other hand, a few of today's high-tension marching drums owe something to the look created by Duplex—as perhaps do recent drum introductions from Peavey. (But what would the percussion industry be without sincere copying?) I hope more information surfaces on this company. They deserve a better fate than near anonymity.

FLAT JACKS
Thinner, Lighter, Louder

From good old Elkhart, Indiana, former home of Leedy, Ludwig & Ludwig, Leedy & Ludwig, and George Way, came a flat-as-a-pancake kind of drum known as the *Flat Jack.* These drums, somewhat similar to shell-less drums available today, were built for both set work and (interestingly) for marching bands.

Each drum, except the snare, had a single head suspended inside a metal ring. Around the ring were a number of tensioning rods that tightened directly in, instead of tightening down.

The advantage for marching bands was that the drums were much lighter than conventional models, and the bass and tenor drums were easy to spin. The advantage of the sets was the low weight and easy portability. The disadvantage was that the products didn't sell and *Flat Jacks* became history, instead of making it.

Flat Jacks weren't successful when they were developed in the mid-'60s—but they foreshadowed similar products introduced more recently.

KENT

Many drummers in the '60s started out playing Kent drums—an American-built product from Kenmore, New York. The drums featured thin maple shells and simply designed die-cast lugs. Kent drum badges were circular and made of metal foil. Holders, strainers, and leg mounts were far from state-of-the-art.

The company imported microphones, amplifiers, and guitars from Japan, put Kent badges on them, and sold them to the drum dealers along with their drums.

Legend has it that drum manufacturing was halted when the son of the owner was killed in a car crash.

Courtesy Rob Cook

The Kent badge

GEORGE B. STONE & SON, INC.
There Are No Better Drums Made

In 1890, Boston music store-owner George B. Stone (father of famed drummer/author George Lawrence Stone) joined a select group of other Boston-based manufacturers of fine percussion instruments: Frank Dodge, Noke & Nicolai, and Harry Bower. The Stone company built its own wood-shell drums and also sold products from other manufacturers, like Ludwig & Ludwig and Walberg & Auge.

Stone & Son's crowning glory was a one-piece maple-shell snare drum known as the *Master Model*. Each drum had separate tension rods that were attached to claws that pulled the hoops down

Stone's Trap Door Bass Drum did double-duty as an instrument and a trap case.

on the heads. The *Master Model* was typically finished in natural maple, stained, or painted black or white. I have one from the late Stone period (1929) that has chrome hardware and is finished in white pearl with cream-colored hoops. It is very striking. Unfortunately (from a collector's point of view), it also has a 3-ply shell as opposed to a solid shell. However, there is a trade-off regarding the look. The age-old problem with solid-shell drums from the 1920s through the '40s is the out-of-round condition that occurs when wood, having been accustomed to being a plank, is bent into a circle. Nature tells it to straighten out and be a plank again. The conflict between nature pulling and hide glue resisting often creates a "flat-tire" look in these drums.

The Stone company lasted into the early 1930s before the manufacturing machinery was put into storage. The same machinery was purchased in 1950 by Ralph Eames, who moved it to Wakefield, Massachusetts—where he used it to build rope-tension drums. In 1978, Joe MacSweeney bought the Eames company, and he now uses the same historic drum-manufacturing equipment that George B. Stone ran so many years before to create Eames custom shells.

FRANK WOLF
The Very Finest and Most Practical Drum So Far
Conceived and Offered

In the 1930s, a New York drummer named Frank Wolf created the 2-to-1 concept. Frank—who opened his drum business in 1910—believed that a snare drum's top head should be a third higher in pitch than the bottom head. He created this sound by placing twelve lugs around the top of each drum and six lugs on the bottom. The wood-shell snare came only in a 6½x14 size. A copper shell with a double bead was also available. The strainer was a uniquely shaped model also used by Rogers. The lugs on the

Courtesy Ned Ingberman, Vintage Drum Center

Frank Wolf's 2-to-1 snare drum

snare drum and tunable tom-toms were tiny metal blocks; bass drums had tube lugs. Frank mentioned a number of well-known endorsers (who were also featured by national manufacturers)—Ray Bauduc, Chick Webb, and Chauncey Morehouse, to name a few. Wolf himself was an early Leedy endorser and is mentioned in three of the twenty-nine *Leedy Topics*.

Prior to World War II, Wolf's store, across the street from Manny's, held an exclusive Slingerland franchise. So perhaps it's not surprising that in the late '70s, Slingerland unearthed Frank's idea. They manufactured a series of snare drums called (guess what?): 2-to-1. Unlike Frank's version, however, these had variety. The drums were available in wood or metal shell with the following sizes: 5x14 in brass, or 6½x14 and 6½x15 in wood or metal. The brass snares were either chrome-plated or just lacquered.

Slingerland had the same success that Wolf had: none. Maybe it's that the 2-to-1 lug system just doesn't *look* right. But the drum world, like fashion, goes through a version of "wide tie…narrow tie."

The Frank Wolf badge

If we just wait a few more years, no doubt someone will introduce the 2-to-1 idea to a generation that has never seen it.

Frank Wolf's store continued to operate through the 1960s, run by his sons Herb and Al. Today, the store, like the 2-to-1 concept, has its place in drum history.

ZICKOS

Zickos were clear acrylic-shell drums that enjoyed popularity in the 1960s. The tom-toms were conventional in size with teardrop-shaped lugs and long extension mounting arms. Due to their length, lugs on mounted toms were offset. Bass drums were deeper than normal and used metal hoops rather than wooden ones.

Zickos snare drums used Ludwig *P85* strainers and *P32* butt plates. I remember seeing Floyd Sneed, the great drummer with Three Dog Night, sitting behind his Zickos drumkit. It was a time of flowered and psychedelic prints, and you could literally see the drummer's wardrobe *through* his drums.

The material used to make acrylic shells was petroleum-based, and the oil crisis of the early '70s played havoc with the prices and availability of acrylic drums. There have been attempts to revive Zickos.

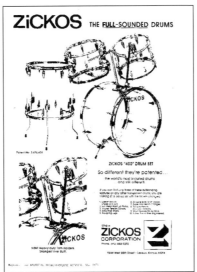

Zickos was a short-lived player among the clear drumset brands.

Chapter 17

Drumheads

Before the invention of *Mylar* by DuPont in the late 1950s, drumheads were made of animal skins. Certain drum companies made their own heads; others bought them from outside sources and/or from competitors. The most common source of drumheads was calfskin, but heads were also made from goat, pig, kangaroo, and sheepskin.

Sheepskin was often advertised as calfskin, but the tissue contained little natural glue and did not wear as well. Goat skins were often found on Latin instruments. Pigskin has a high fat content and was used in tacked-head situations because of its thickness—so it was the first kind used on toms. At that point, they were not tunable. Kangaroo was a turn-of-the-century choice.

Calfskin came in three grades. The first, considered plump and tightly fibered, was from milk-fed beef or veal calf. Grade two came from animals fed processed feed, buttermilk, or skim milk by farmers. Grade three came from pasture grazers. While all three were of good quality, the first, veal calf, was professionally recommended.

Drumhead buyers from the various drum companies visited stockyards daily to buy fresh hides. Chicago's preeminence in the meat-packing industry was of prime importance to the development of the Slingerland and Ludwig & Ludwig companies. The skins were cleaned, bleached, and cured in refrigerated rooms. After curing, skins were stretched on frames and then shaved.

Final cutting, buffing, and shaving of the heads occurred before the last inspection. Then the heads were tucked into metal or wooden hoops, depending on the brand.

The smell was terrible in the tanneries, and the process attracted vermin—but the country's drummers needed calf heads. Slunk heads were used for the snare side. These were the skins of unborn calves and were thin, therefore perfect for the snares.

Many snare drums of the '20s and '30s have heater units installed. A rod could be heated by the current from the closest electrical outlet. The heat kept a damp head from becoming mushy.

Today, collectors may find a certain drum that cannot use off-the-shelf plastic heads. Usually the diameter of the drum is just over "regulation" size. When calf was king many players tucked their own heads, and an eighth of an inch here or there was never a problem. Collectors can do almost the same thing by sending a tracing of

Stretching skin heads in the Leedy factory, circa 1923

Tucking heads on flesh hoops

the diameter of the drum or the flesh hoop (the wood or metal hoop onto which the head was tucked) to Steve Palansky at United Rawhide in Chicago, or to one of the plastic head manufacturers. (Just be patient; it can take months.)

Each of the vintage drumhead manufacturers labeled its heads with ink stamp logos. Normally there were different marks at various price points. Ludwig & Ludwig, for example, had Bill Senior's signature for its top line. Thick heads called the *Ludwig Whitecalf* series used a trademark of a side view of a calf. The slunk head series—using a drawing of a cow's head with a crown—was called *Ludwig Crown Brand.*

From 1960 on most drums were fitted with *Mylar* heads, and one by one the calfskin head manufacturers went out of business. Today, only United Rawhide is still making heads like the craftsmen of Leedy and Ludwig & Ludwig did seventy years ago.

Ludwig drumhead logos illustrating the various quality levels of heads

Chapter 18

Most Collectible Snare Drums 1920-1969

This chapter presents a listing of those snare drums that have become the most sought-after by (and most valuable to) collectors in recent years. The listings indicate the brand and model of each drum, and sometimes contain a comment about specific details to be aware of when considering the purchase of such a drum.

5¹/₂x14 Camco Aristocrat
(shown: white marine pearl finish, circa 1966)

3¹/₂x14 Camco Jazz Model
(shown: white marine pearl finish, circa 1963)

5x14 Fibes SFT690
(shown: black acrylic shell, circa 1968)

Photo by Mark Hamon

6¹/₂x14 Billy Gladstone
(shown: bird's-eye maple shell with gold plating, circa 1951)

6¹/₂x14 Gretsch Gladstone
(shown: oriental pearl finish, circa 1939)

5¹/₂x14 Gretsch Name Band
75th Anniversary Model
(shown: diamond sparkle finish, circa 1958)

4x14 Gretsch Progressive Jazz
(shown: starlight sparkle finish, circa 1959)

4x14 Leedy (Indianapolis) Black Elite
(shown: black elite engraved nickel finish
over brass shell, circa 1926)

5x14 Leedy (Indianapolis) Professional
(metal shell)
(shown: nickel over brass shell,
circa 1925 [top] and 1927 [bottom])

6x14 Leedy (Indianapolis) Professional
(solid walnut shell)
(shown: white enamel finish [top],
Tudor walnut finish [bottom], circa 1927)

6½x14 Leedy (Elkhart) Broadway
(through X-lug period)
(shown: solid maple shell,
white marine pearl finish, circa 1935)

5½x14 Leedy (Chicago) Shelly Manne
(shown: white marine pearl finish,
circa 1965)

4x14 Leedy & Ludwig Broadway New Era
(shown: white marine pearl finish,
circa 1951)

5x14 Ludwig Supraphonic (brass shell)
(shown: chrome over brass shell,
circa 1961)

4x14 Ludwig Downbeat
(shown: silver sparkle finish, circa 1965)

6½x14 Ludwig Super Classic
(with Classic strainer)
(shown: blue sparkle finish, circa 1967)

4x14 Ludwig & Ludwig (Chicago) Deluxe
(also known as Black Beauty)
(shown: black nickel finish over brass shell,
circa 1924)

5½x14 Ludwig & Ludwig (Chicago)
Super Ludwig
(solid wood shell)
(shown: white Avalon pearl finish, circa 1929)

5¹/₂x14 Ludwig & Ludwig (Elkhart)
Silver Anniversary Deluxe
(shown: black engraved finish over brass shell,
circa 1935)

5¹/₂x14 Ludwig (Elkhart) Silver Anniversary
(shown: chrome over brass, circa 1935)

5x14 Rogers Dyna-Sonic
(wood shell)
(shown: champagne sparkle, circa 1965)

5¹/₂x14 Slingerland Artist
(solid shell; Zoomatic strainer)
(shown: white marine pearl finish, circa 1965)

6¹/₂x14 Slingerland Radio King
(3-point strainer; clam-shell strainers
on similar drums can be finicky)
(shown: white marine pearl with nickel
plating, circa 1938)

6x14 George B. Stone Master Model
(shown: white marine pearl finish, circa 1930)

5¹/₂x14 George Way Aristocrat
(shown: red sparkle finish, circa 1959)

6¹/₂x14 WFL (early) Twin Strainer
(with cast lugs)
(shown: white marine pearl finish,
circa 1939)

6x14 WFL (later) Super Classic
(with Classic strainer)
(shown: white marine pearl, circa 1952)

Chapter 19

Distinguishing Features

It's not always easy to pinpoint the exact age, model—or even brand—of a vintage or historic drum. But there are certain features that distinguish one drum from another. The photos and notes presented in this chapter illustrate many of those features, in the hope that they will help drummers and collectors to better identify exactly what they're looking at when examining a potential "collector's item."

CAMCO

Badges

Winged badge, 1962-1969

Oval badge, 1969-1970

Hoops

High-collar hoop, 1962-1970 (also shown: *Aristocrat* lug, same period)

Lugs

Tuxedo lug, 1962-1970

Strainers

Aristocrat, 1962-1970

Economy, 1962-1970

Note: *Parallel* (cylindrical "Super" strainer) and *Tuxedo* (trapezoidal-shaped with "Camco" stamp) were also made, but are extremely rare.

DUPLEX

Note: All hardware other than lugs was fairly generic for the period between 1900 and 1940.

Lugs

External tube lug (as opposed to internal lugs used on *Spirit Of St. Louis* model). This design goes back to the 1880s; Duplex was the first company to have separate-tension lugs.

FIBES

Badges

Fibes badge, 1965-1970

Hoops

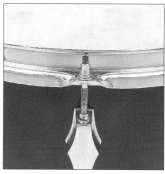

Triple-flanged hoop, 1965-1970

Lugs

Fibes lug, 1965-1970

Strainers

SFT 90 strainer, 1965-1970

GRETSCH

Badges

Round badge, 1920s-1969
(Later badges are outside the
timeline of this book.)

Hoops

Single-flanged hoop, pre-1930s

Double-flanged hoop, pre-1930s

Note: Single- and double-flanged
hoops were fairly generic and virtually identical to those used by
most other drum companies during this period.

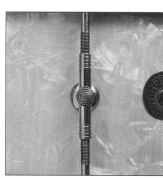

Die-cast double-flanged hoop,
mid-1930s through mid-1950s

Hoops

Die-cast triple-flanged hoop,
mid-1950s-1969

Lugs

Note: Early tube lugs were generic and similar to all others used on
drums prior to the mid-1930s.

Broadkaster (a.k.a. "Rocket") lug,
mid-1930s-1949

Gretsch-Gladstone tube lug,
1939-1945

Small modern Broadkaster lug (for
double-row separate-tension
snares and tom-toms), 1950-1969

Long modern Broadkaster lug (for
center-mount snares and tom-
toms), 1950-1969

Progressive Jazz lug, 1950-1969

Clips

Clips connected tension rods to
hoops on Dixieland and other
inexpensive models using straight
hoops, 1920s-1960s.

Strainers

Note: From 1935 through 1945
Gretsch Broadkaster snare drums
used Radio King strainers by
Slingerland. See the Slingerland
section for illustration.

Gretsch Gladstone strainer,
1939-1945

Micro-Sensitive strainer, mid-1950s-1969

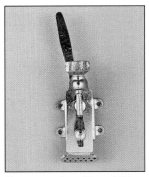

Renown strainer (6- and 8-lug models), mid-1950s-1969

LEEDY
(Indianapolis)

Badges

Note: Leedy used no badges; logos were engraved on hoops and strainer knobs.

Hoops

Note: Generic straight and single-flanged hoops were used from the 1920s-1950.

Double-channeled hoop (on *Multi-Model* snare drum), 1920-1924

Double-flanged hoop (on *Floating Head* snare drum), 1924-1950

Lugs

Clips connected tension rods to hoops on *Dixieland* and other inexpensive models using straight hoops, 1920s-1960s.

Four-hole "semi-self-aligning" lug, 1925-1929

Clips

Leedy clip, 1920s-1950s

Inverted clip (used on low-line snare drums), 1930s-1950s

Strainers

Utility strainer, 1912-1950

Marvel strainer, 1926

Presto two-hole, 1924-1928

Speedway two-hole, 1926-1929

Speedway four-hole, 1929-1935 (later known as *Broadway Standard*; first series used on Leedy [Elkhart] drums)

LEEDY
(Elkhart)

Badges

Brass badge, 1930-1948

Blue badge, 1949-1950

Hoops

Note: Same as Leedy (Indianapolis); no *Multi-Channel* hoops

Lugs

X lug, 1930-1938

Streamlined (a.k.a. "Beavertail") lug, 1938-1950 (Also shown: *Broadway Standard* second series strainer, 1933-1937)

Clips

Note: See Leedy (Indianapolis)

Strainers

Broadway Parallel, first series, 1930-1935

Broadway Parallel, second series, 1933-1936

Broadway Parallel, third series, 1937-1945

Broadway Standard, third series, 1938-1950

LEEDY & LUDWIG
AND
LEEDY (CHICAGO)

Badges

Leedy & Ludwig badge, 1950-1954

Leedy (Chicago) brass oval badge, 1955-1956

Leedy (Chicago) blue oval badge, 1957-1970

Hoops

Note: For Leedy & Ludwig, see Leedy (Elkhart) straight, single-flanged, and double-flanged hoops. For Leedy (Chicago), see Slingerland.

Lugs

Note: Leedy & Ludwig high-end drums used Leedy "Beavertail" lugs; low-end drums used Ludwig tube lugs and *Imperial* lugs. Leedy (Chicago) continued the use of Leedy "Beavertail" lugs and also used new center-mount lugs, as on the Shelly Manne model (see chapter 18).

Clips

Note: For Leedy & Ludwig and Leedy (Chicago) clips, see Leedy (Elkhart).

Strainers

Note: For Leedy & Ludwig high-end drums, see the Leedy (Elkhart) *Broadway Standard* third series. For low-end drums, see the Ludwig & Ludwig *Pioneer*. Leedy (Chicago) drums carried on the Leedy (Elkhart) *Broadway Standard* third series, and also used the *Instant* strainer (see the Slingerland *Rapid* strainer) and the *Professional* strainer (see the Slingerland *Radio King 3-Point* strainer).

L&S

Badges

L&S badge, 1933-38

Hoops

Note: L&S used generic straight, single-flanged, and double-flanged hoops

Lugs

Note: Early L&S drums used generic tube lugs.

L&S cast lug (*Dictator* snare drum), 1933-38 (Also shown: *Nokut* snare strainer, 1933-38)

Clips

Note: See Leedy

Strainers

Note: Besides the *Nokut* model, L&S drums featured four other strainer designs. Photos are virtually non-existent due to the rarity of the drums themselves—owing, in turn, to the company's lack of success.

LUDWIG DRUM CO.

Badges

"Transition" badge, 1960

"Keystone" badge, with serial number, 1964-1969 (1961-1963 badges were identical but carried no serial number.)

Hoops

Triple-flanged hoop, 1955-1969

Lugs

Improved *Imperial* lug, with swivel nut, 1959-1969

Classic lug, 1955-1969 (For small *Classic* lug, see WFL)

Piccolo lug, 1955-1969

Strainers

Note: For the *P70 Pioneer* strainer see Ludwig & Ludwig.

Classic strainer, 1955-1969 (Some holdovers from WFL were used until the inventory was depleted.)

P83 strainer, 1955-1969

Super Sensitive strainer, 1960-1969

LUDWIG & LUDWIG

Badges

Early Ludwig & Ludwig drums had the name engraved in the hoops or stamped into the metal shells. The first attempt at a badge, around 1910, saw it mounted behind the strainer. This method was quickly discarded.

Brass badge, late 1920s

Enamel badge, later 1920s

Hoops

Note: Early drums used generic straight and single-flanged hoops.

Double-flanged hoop, early 1930s-1950

Lugs

Note: Generic tube lugs were used from 1909 through 1950.

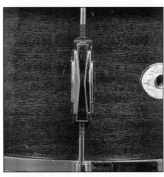

Original *Imperial* lug, 1935-1950

Clips

Clip for straight or single-flanged hoops (*Black Beauty* shown), 1912-1950

Strainers

Combination strainer, 1909-1917

Pioneer strainer, 1917-1950

Note: The *Professional* model was a *Pioneer* with an extended handle that sat behind the knurled knob.

Parallel strainer, first series, 1927-1935

Parallel strainer, second series, 1936-1945

Standard strainer, 1936-1950

ROGERS

Badges

Eagle badge, pre-1950s (used until supply exhausted)

First script logo, 1958-1959

Second script logo, 1960-1969

Dyna-Sonic badge, 1962-1969

Hoops

Note: Generic single- and double-flanged hoops were used from the 1920s through the 1960s.

Triple-flanged high-collar hoop, mid-1950s-1969

Lugs

Note: Generic tube lugs were used from the 1920s through the 1940s. An early version of the drawn-brass lug (1940-1950) had an "R" in the center of the spine.

Drawn-brass lug, intermediate version, 1950-1958

Final drawn-brass lug ("Bread & Butter"), with ridge in center, 1959-1964

Beavertail lug, 1964-1969

Clips

Note: See Gretsch

Strainers

Note: In the 1930s Rogers used Slingerland *3-Point* strainers, as well as the same strainer used by Frank Wolf. See Slingerland.

Compact strainer, 1955-1962

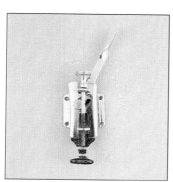

Orchestra (a.k.a. *Universal*) strainer, 1960-1965

Holiday strainer, 1962-1965

Note: *Orchestra* and *Holiday* strainers were replaced in the late 1960s by *Sta-Tite* and *Bantam* models. Both of these were cut-down versions of the *Swiv-O-Matic*.

Swiv-O-Matic strainer, 1963-1969

SLINGERLAND

Badges

Note: Early drums had the Slingerland name engraved in the hoops or stamped into the metal shell.

"Cloud" badge, mid-1930s-1945 (Prior to WWII the badge was made of brass; during the war it was aluminum.)

Post-WWII badge, 1945-1950

Black and brass Chicago badge, 1950-1959

Black and brass Niles badge, 1960-1969
(A second assembly plant was located in Shelbyville, Tennessee during this period. Badges from that plant are oval in brass and maroon.)

Black and silver Niles badge, 1970

Hoops

Note: Generic straight and single-flanged hoops were used from 1928 through 1969.

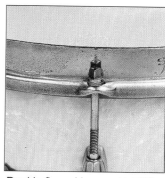

Double-flanged hoop, mid-1930s-1954

Triple-flanged "Stick Saver" hoop, 1955-1969

Lugs

Note: Generic tube lugs were used from 1928 to 1945. The *Streamlined* lug was used from the mid-1930s through the early 1950s. (See the *3-Point* strainer photo in this section.)

Super Streamlined (a.k.a. "Beavertail") lug, 1940-early 1950s.

Sound King lug, 1955-1969

Clips

Note: See Leedy for examples of early clips.

Clips in the late 1930s had a unique wide base.

Strainers

Shur Grip strainer, late 1920s-mid-1930s

Speedy Shur Hold or *Radio King* (a.k.a. *3-Point* and *Krupa*) strainer, 1928-1969
(Also used by Rogers and Gretsch. Later versions had one-piece throw arms.)

Super Strainer (a.k.a. "Clamshell"), 1940-1960

Zoomatic strainer, circa 1960
(Replacement for *Super Strainer*)

Rapid strainer, 1960-1969

WFL

Badges

Lyre badge, 1937-1938

Final WFL "Keystone" badge, 1938-1955

Hoops

Note: Generic straight and single-flanged hoops were used from 1936 through 1949.

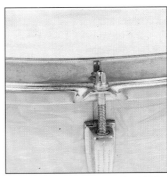
Triple-flanged hoop, 1936-1955

Lugs

Note: Generic tube lugs were used from 1936 through 1945.

Zephyr lug, 1937-1947

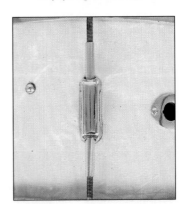
Streamlined lug, 1937-1946

Classic lug, 1947-1955

Note: A piccolo lug similar to Ludwig's but plainer in design was used by WFL from 1950 to 1955.

Hoops

Note: Generic straight and single-flanged hoops were used from 1936 through 1949.

Clips

Note: See Leedy.

Strainers

Twin strainer, 1938-1945
(The *P35* was a single version of this strainer.)

P83 strainer, 1940-1955

Classic strainer, 1947-1955

GEORGE WAY

Badges

Winged badge, 1957-1961

Hoops

Note: Single-flanged hoops were used on some models from 1957 through 1961.

Triple-flanged hoop, 1957-1961

Lugs

Aristocrat lug, 1957-1961

Note: For the *Tuxedo* lug, see Camco.

Clips

Note: See Leedy.

Strainers

Precision (later *Paramount*, still later *Aristocrat*) strainer, 1957-1961

Glossary

ArtGold: Slingerland metal finish; see "nobby gold."

Badge: Typically, a brass identification plate that encircles a vent hole. Each manufacturer's badge had a distinct shape. The badges of World War II were usually made of aluminum. Logos were accompanied by the cities of manufacture.

Butt Plate: The metal (or wood during World War II) clamp attached to a snare drum directly opposite the strainer. Used to hold the snares while the strainer tightens, loosens, engages, or disengages them.

Casing: Another term for tension casing or lug.

Center Bead: The contoured middle section of many metal snare drums. Originally seen on Ludwig & Ludwig drums starting in 1914, center beads were later adopted by other brands.

Claw: The original name for the large hooks that tightened on the hoops of bass drums. Replaced by the double claw.

Clip: An alternate name for a small hook used to receive a threaded rod that tightened into a tube or lug. The clip had a curved shape that pulled down a flat or single-flanged hoop. Used through the '60s on low-end models but replaced largely in the '30s by double- and triple-flanged hoops on premium-model snares and tom-toms.

Counterhoop: Another name for the metal or wood hoops also called "rims" on the top and bottom sides of snares and tom-toms.

Deluxe: Ludwig & Ludwig metal finish; see "nobby gold."

Double Claw: The modern bass drum claw. A tube-like center section receives a T-rod or key-operated tension rod that screws into a casing. On each side of the center tube are large hooks to hold the bass drum hoops. Each company designed its own double claw.

Double-Flanged Hoop: The first hoops to replace single-flanged models. The second flange covered the flesh hoop of a drumhead and allowed tension rods to pass through the hoop.

Flat Hoop: The earliest steel counterhoops, used with clips. Replaced by single-flanged hoops. Retained through the '60s on lowest-cost snare drums.

Flesh Hoop: The metal or wooden rim onto which calf heads were tucked.

Klondyke Gold: Rogers metal finish; see "nobby gold."

Lug: The most common name for a tension casing. The modern lug, which is fully self-aligning, started with Leedy in 1930, and was called the X lug. The most popular pre-modern lug is the tube lug, a simple but attractive model. Since they do not have a self-aligning feature, tube lugs can be stripped. Inside the modern lug are two threaded lug nuts with a spring between them. (Springs are sometimes replaced by plastic inserts.)

Muffler: Originally, a name given to the strainer (e.g., muffler-strainer), the muffler was a felt circle or square pulled up against the underside of the batter head by a tightening knob or lever.

Nobby Gold: Leedy's name for a metal finish that employed a gold tinted lacquer applied to polished brass. (Other brands used their respective names for the same type of finish.) Initially, the bright finish rivaled gold plating at a lower cost. But time darkens the finish, and it can wear off. All nobby gold, art gold, deluxe, and Klondyke gold parts should be cleaned using a light oil like *3-in-1 Oil*. Never use hot water!

Rod: The threaded metal bolt that tightens drumheads. Most have raised square surfaces that fit into drumkeys. Early rods from Leedy had a slot head. Other companies had rods with hexagonal-shaped heads. Modern rods have 12-24 threads. At one point, early lugs were referred to as rods. That description encompassed one lug and two threaded rods as a complete unit.

Single-Flanged Hoop: A hoop with a distinct L shape at its base that pushed down on the flesh hoop. The L or single flange also created a base on which the clips would rest.

Strainer: The mechanism used to tighten and engage the snares.

Triple-Flanged Hoops: The modern drum hoop. It was created at WFL when Cecil Strupe took a double-flanged hoop and bent the top outward in an effort to reduce stick breakage.

Vent Hole: A hole drilled into a drum shell to allow the passage of air and thereby enlarge the sound. All snare and bass drums had vent holes, but many tom-toms did not—even into the '60s. Most companies placed their logo badges around vent holes.